THE
INCLUSIVE
ORGANIZATION

THE

INCLUSIVE

ORGANIZATION

Real Solutions,
Impactful Change,
and Meaningful
Diversity

NETTA JENKINS

WILEY

For general information on our other products and services or for technical support, please contact our Customer Care Department within the United States at (800) 762-2974, outside the United States at (317) 572-3993 or fax (317) 572-4002.

Wiley also publishes its books in a variety of electronic formats. Some content that appears in print may not be available in electronic formats. For more information about Wiley products, visit our web site at www.wiley.com.

Library of Congress Cataloging-in-Publication Data is Available:

ISBN 9781119910138 (Cloth)
ISBN 9781119910176 (ePub)
ISBN 9781119910244 (ePDF)

Cover Design: Wiley
Cover Image: © ART PAL/Shuttterstock

I dedicate this book to my mother, Nellie Gaye; my two children, Taton and Talon Jenkins; my dear husband, Eric Jenkins; my bonus son, Eric Jenkins Jr; my supportive siblings, Tyrone Gaye, Decontee Gaye, and Jonathan Gaye; and my dad, Samuel Gaye. My mom looked me in the eyes as a young child and told me that I had the power to change the world. I remember looking at her confused, wondering if that was truly possible. But with those words my mom gifted me the power of confidence. She empowered me to take up space and prepare to not only take a seat at the table but to bring along some extra seats as well. I'm ever blessed to have a mother who instilled in me the belief that I would affect and change the world. My children, currently two and three years old, motivate me with an unparalleled drive. They have taught me to be patient and taught me about unconditional love. I am still trying to figure out what true balance means and looks like for me, but through my children I have learned how to create opportunities for multiple dreams to be realized. None of which would be possible without my mighty village which has always stepped in to support both my family and professional endeavors, whether or not I asked for help. I am so grateful to each one of you for helping me to bring my dreams to life. This one is for all of us.

Contents

Introduction

I REMEMBER being a young girl, riding my bike down the peaceful tree-lined street I grew up on in quiet Rhode Island. We were one of the only Black families in our neighborhood, but I never really noticed or thought about it as a child. I remember playing with my best friend who lived just upstairs from my family. The two of us were inseparable; we spent our days biking around our neighborhood, looking for dinosaur fossils, and laughing until our bellies hurt. My childhood was full of moments like these—innocent, free, and light. But when I was seven years old, my bubble of innocence burst, as I was exposed to an uglier side of our society that would stick with me for the rest of my life. My family had just moved into a single-family home, still in the same town I'd lived in since I was a baby. My mother and I were standing in our new yard when a white woman walked right up to my mother and spat directly on her face.

"Blacks don't belong in my neighborhood," she violently hissed at my mother. I stood frozen, watching the woman's yellow phlegm drip down my mother's face. My mother calculated her options; to this day I can still see her doing the mental math on how to get us both safely out of the situation. In tandem, without saying a word, we turned around and walked into our home. We both went to sleep that night crying.

I share this story with you to explain why my life and career have followed the path that they have. This incident ended up stoking a deep desire to understand how the brain works and why people behave as they do. This curiosity led me to major in communications and minor in leadership with a keen focus on behavioral psychology. After going on to get my MBA, I joined the corporate workforce and started working as a diversity, equity, and inclusion (DEI) specialist for all sorts of organizations, from Fortune 500 companies to smaller startups to passionate entrepreneurs looking to start a business. Through my education and professional experience, I've been able to merge the work I've done my entire life with what I've learned through my own lived experiences. This foundation has helped inform the DEI framework I have developed to help organizations of all sizes and stages build truly inclusive and equitable practices.

This book is an interactive guide to building an inclusive organization. It will help you operate and coach others on how to specifically operate from a DEI lens. You may be a CEO or founder, a board member, an individual contributor, or someone wanting to practice allyship with impact. No matter who you are, there will always be more to learn and ways to enhance your practice. As the workforce becomes more flexible to accommodate our fast and dynamic lives, employees care more and more about organizational practices and culture. They, understandably, want to know that they will be supported in navigating their personal responsibilities while pursuing their professional aspirations.

I have always firmly believed that people are at the core of any business. Despite our immense technological advancements, people remain and will continue to remain at the core of any business. Organizations should always invest in their people and remember that the best ways to do so are by keeping their people interested, informed, and inspired. If organizations can commit to doing this with accountability and explicit metrics, then together we can start a DEI movement.

As a kid I started a DEI movement by challenging my teachers to include different narratives in their coursework. Even from a young age, I never believed in a single, unequivocal, and uncompromising view. I always felt that there were multiple perspectives that all deserved to be heard. As an adult, I want to help bring those voices into the limelight. I want to provide guidance to those who want to listen and a megaphone for those who wish to be heard. And that's exactly what I plan to do with this book.

This book does not seek to point fingers or assign blame. This book is for the reader who says, "I want to take action, but I don't quite know how." It's for the reader who says, "I have been taking action, but I know I can take it a step further." It's even for the reader who says, "I don't know what DEI is, but I want to learn more." No matter which reader you most resonate with, I urge you to seize this opportunity and use this book to create a DEI movement. Each chapter will walk you through a different segment of my DEI framework and include worksheets that provide an opportunity for self-reflection and self-action. Really spend time with these worksheets, explore each topic in depth, and think about how you can apply what you've learned to your current situation. And remember, movements are successful when they have the power of the people. You do not have to start this movement alone. Grab your friends and colleagues, your leaders and mentors, and read through this book together. Share what you learn, ignite each other's inspiration, and come together to work on these areas together. So, if you are ready to officially start a movement with me, then take a photo of you and this book, share it on LinkedIn with the hashtag *#DEIMOVEMENT*, and tag me, Netta Jenkins. Together, we can power this DEI movement. Let's jump in; the water has never been warmer.

1

Decoding Human Behavior

When was the last time you found yourself in a blood-boiling disagreement with a partner or friend that evokes a high level of anxiety every time you think about it? You picked your battle that day and decided not to say anything. Why? Maybe you were worried about retribution, maybe you didn't want to be labeled as "difficult" or "confrontational," or maybe you simply did not have the emotional capacity that day to allow an argument to get instigated. Or perhaps you did say something, and in turn were completely disregarded. This culminated in your anger and disappointment growing and festering until one day you reached your limit and finally left that relationship. This is how a portion of the population feels on a daily basis: forced to withstand wave after wave of aggression, even aggression masquerading as friendliness.

When such actions continue to go unchecked, people will reach a point at which they will leave relationships and situations that do not give them the grace to be heard or supported. When people try to speak up and are disregarded, a growing tension starts and festers. So how can we equip ourselves with the tools to both actively listen and advocate for ourselves to be heard? Please lean on me as we begin our journey of exploring the intricacies of building a truly inclusive organization, but before we can start to construct solutions, we must take a moment and understand how these problems arose in the first place. I ask that you remain open-minded and open-hearted as you read some of the historical pieces I'm going to explore in this chapter. I assure you that I am committed to growing a relationship with you on your journey to unfolding all the pieces within this book.

I believe that this journey requires a renewed cultivation of our limbic system—the part of the brain that enables each of us to understand our behavioral and emotional responses. This limbic cultivation may not always feel pleasant, and there will be parts of this book that will touch on painful topics and may evoke feelings of vulnerability. I want you to know that even as I write these words, I am aware of the effort it may take at times to relive or uncover some of the uglier parts of our history, but that I am here with you every step of the way. Let us hold each other's hand through this process and come out on the other side, stronger and together.

History of Race

In 1449, Spain passed an official proclamation that would later be known as the first set of discriminatory laws based on race. This edict would lay the foundation for the Spanish Inquisition, in which racism was fully legalized and culminated in the murder and expulsion of hundreds of thousands of Spanish Jews, Muslims, and Protestants. While I understand the Spanish Inquisition to be the first recorded instance of sustained and strategic violence on the basis of race and "othering," the tactics of racial oppression and discrimination that were conceived in the 15th century gave birth to what I call *the Great Divergence*. All of the atrocities we have seen follow the Inquisition—from genocide to slavery to internment camps to the Holocaust—demonstrate that these "historical" actions may not be as behind us as many would like to believe. People generally would like to think that we have made some massive improvements, that our society now is eons beyond the hate and violence of previous centuries, as illustrated in the black-and-white photographs documenting the 1960s Civil Rights movement. But the first in-color photos were developed in France in 1907, and yet all of the powerful photographs depicting the resilience of the Civil Rights era were purposefully printed in black and white and are still distributed as such, pushing a false narrative that the days of bus bombing, police violence, and white people spitting in the faces of Black folks are far gone. But had Dr. Martin Luther King Jr. not been assassinated, or Anne Frank not been sent by Nazis to perish in a concentration camp, they could both be alive today, and would have still been younger than the late, vivacious Betty White. See, although it is far easier and far more comfortable to let history stay in the past, we must confront the painful and uncomfortable truth—that this suffering, this discrimination, this violence, are still very much embedded into daily life, even in the 21st century, and we can see it everywhere, if we are willing to open our eyes and look. From playgrounds to understocked grocery stores to overflowing prisons to our own workplaces, we are still living every day with the legacy of some of our most painful historic miscarriages.

But this book is not meant to be a history lesson. This book is meant to act as a guide, to provide you, the reader, with a specific toolkit to equip you to really create the change you want to see in your workplace. Maybe you are currently a leader of a huge corporation looking to help lead a cultural shift within your organization. Maybe you are a leader of a startup wanting to ensure diversity, equity, and inclusion (DEI) is proactively embedded in the infant stages of your organizations. Maybe you are currently navigating the workplace and struggling with the weight of feeling othered or unseen by your fellow colleagues, or maybe you are someone who is simply curious to learn more about DEI and understand why it's been such a point of conversation in the last few years. Wherever you are in your journey, whatever perspective you are bringing or guidance you are seeking, this book will—I hope—provide you with the context to truly understand and verbalize what you are seeing and experiencing, and impart on you the practical and actionable steps to empower yourself and your colleagues to bring forth and sustain impactful solutions within your workplace.

The Great Divergence

And that brings me back to the Great Divergence. The last few years have sent the world into an upheaval in a way that we've never seen before. Never before has technology tied communities across the globe so closely together with social media platforms updating us on every occurrence across country and continental lines. Along with constant access to information, we are also given constant insight into everyone's opinion on the information we are receiving.

What we are seeing across the board is that there seems to be a strong sense of division. People are feeling polarized, and we've felt that gap reverberate from the family dining table to the company conference table.

It used to be commonplace to differentiate the outside world from the workplace. Professionalism seemingly encompassed a strong need to leave politics at the door. It wasn't professional to discuss certain topics; the workplace was for work, as simple as that. However, coming off of multiple years in which we were isolated out of necessity for safety, those lines have become heavily blurred. It is no longer possible to draw those strong boundaries of global events, personal experiences, and the professional workplace. From folks who lost their entire source of income due to the pandemic and were unable to work, to other industries that switched to operating fully remote, our homes became the physical space in which every part of life happened. From an influx of news about hundreds of thousands of lives lost to the insidious coronavirus, to people flooding the streets in outrage refusing to be silenced as we watched documented murder after murder, to a political insurrection that blatantly challenged our country's pillar of democracy, it has been an incredibly scary and challenging world to navigate. However, even in the midst of this global calamity, when it felt like we just needed to stand still and fully process what we were seeing, time kept ticking and the Earth kept turning. Businesses were doing their best to stay afloat, governments did their best to keep morale high and assure the public that our economies would survive. Unemployment skyrocketed, and those fortunate enough to work in industries that were able to weather the shift to remote work took on the new and unique burden of attempting to maintain a sense of normalcy in a world that felt like it was anything but.

As a DEI executive, I have seen a recurring theme across companies both large and small: there is a divided experience that is informing a divided understanding. We can no longer afford to pretend that this divide doesn't exist. In fact, I have seen the overwhelmingly positive potential that comes when a company chooses to address this divide head on and create a space for their employees to connect in a deeper and more meaningful way than ever before. It's certainly not to say that it was the pandemic that exacerbated the Great Divergence, but more so it removed the niceties that shrouded a divide that has existed for a very long time and has made plain the urgency with which we must address the situation.

So what exactly is this Great Divergence? I define it as the divide that separates individuals into two groups—the first group feels like the discrimination of today is a much improved version of the discrimination of the past, that we are living in much safer and fairer times and therefore there really isn't a need for a strong shift in how we understand and address inequities. And the other group? Well, they disagree.

It is within this tension that the Great Divergence remains. Although the world does indeed look different than it did half a century ago, take just a single step closer, examine societal structures with a slightly keener eye, and we can clearly see the complex discriminative structure of accessible opportunity, power, and protection that is interwoven into the fabric of daily life, and one that our workplaces are by no means exempt from. This structure leads to very stark and distinct experiences for folks who come from systemically overlooked populations. *Systemically overlooked populations* refers to populations who are affected by methods or systems that intentionally disrupt their access to opportunity. I define *systemically overlooked* to include individuals who identify as Black+, Latinx+, Asian+, Indigenous+, as well as intersectional layers that include women, LGBTQIA+, veterans, caregivers, and those who are differently abled. Each of these groups is faced with navigating their own unique set of challenges that have their own historical and social context. I will delve into this further in Chapter 2. Individuals who do not identify as part of a systemically overlooked population will be referred to as "advantaged populations" from this point on.

Sadly, this discriminative structure can manifest in many ways in the workplace. It can look like exclusion from opportunities, getting passed over for promotions, having to navigate the necessity of code-switching, dealing with stereotyped expectations, not being given the same benefit of the doubt that other colleagues receive, massive discrepancies in pay parity across gender and ethnicity, or companies becoming increasingly homogenous as you move up the company structure. This list is by no means exhaustive, as the nuances of how discriminative structures play out in the workplace can be very layered.

The last thing I want to do is paint this as an issue of good versus bad. There are so many complex interactions at play that can shape a person's understanding that it is far too simple, and, honestly, irresponsible, to simply label a segment of the population as malicious or ill-intentioned. Although there is a small group of individuals who unfortunately may be, the vast majority of people are well-intentioned and would never want to actively harm another person—they just might not fully understand how or why their well-intentioned actions could end up having a harmful impact. To really reach a place of genuine and forthright self-reflection and self-accountability will more than likely be an uncomfortable process. It is uncomfortable to sit with the understanding that despite your honest and true effort, there could be some painful consequences of a good intent. It is imperative, however, that in conducting these conversations, we operate from a place of compassion and patience because, more often than not, people really do care. In my work, I have seen the strongest impact and the most progress come from people who are welcomed into the conversation, with all the nuances and complexities they carry. As we start to really listen to people and learn who they are—what motivates them, what scares them, what makes them feel connected to those around them—that is where we will find the solution to bridging the Great Divergence.

So why would someone find themselves of the opinion that discrimination is not alive and thriving? There could be a multitude of reasons, starting with it's simply a more comfortable interpretation. But we have to come to terms with the fact that the ability to feel comfortable is itself a privilege, because there are so many others who, despite their best efforts, cannot even pretend to be comfortable in so many of their interactions. Going a little bit deeper, maybe people are afraid to feel burdened with guilt about the experiences so many overlooked populations have. Maybe they reject that they carry responsibility for their ancestors' actions, that they shouldn't have to be accountable for actions that predated them by hundreds of years. However, how can one blatantly reject the negative consequences of their ancestors' actions while they simultaneously enjoy the positive consequences of those very same actions? We can no longer allow a partial recognition of history or regale only these stories that are written from the perspective of the victor. If the "winners" write the history books, how much of the full story is getting omitted? It is an uncomfortable truth, but a truth nonetheless, that we are in a complex discriminatory war that is fought by systemically overlooked populations. The single constant is that white people, even well-intentioned white people, remain at the helm of this power structure.

This can be a disagreeable statement for people to sit with. In fact, maybe you even feel a slight churn in your stomach or a rebuttal bubbling up to your lips as you read these words. I don't say this to be divisive. I say this to be direct and frank, because only through explicitly naming the issue can we begin to build an inclusive and successful solution. To continue in that vein, it is imperative that all leaders, especially those who do not identify as part of a systemically overlooked population, take a moment of genuine and uninhibited self-reflection, because we have come to know that the dynamics in the real world very much bleed into dynamics in the workplace. Leaders in any organization can wittingly or unwittingly perpetuate these power structures, and the impact of this can be immense. By unknowingly upholding this power structure, the Great Divergence continues to oppress overlooked populations and inequity persists.

Bridging the Great Divergence

So how exactly can leaders address and begin to bridge this divergence? Just as with the problem, the solution can take form in many different ways. We will break this down further in Chapter 6, but it can look like creating policies to hold your organization and the organizations you work with accountable in maintaining diverse retention at all levels; providing leadership and decision-making opportunities to individuals from overlooked populations; or even coming to the understanding that sometimes the most impactful thing you can do is empty your seat and offer access to the resources, network, and skill set that helped you get to where you are today to another individual from an overlooked population who can bring in the perspective to truly help your organization evolve to the next level.

I want to take a second and examine an example of an advantaged leader who took active steps to create an inclusive solution to addressing the racial gap that he noticed within the board of his company. Alexis Ohanian, cofounder of Reddit and husband of Serena Williams, resigned from his role as Reddit board member 15 years after cofounding the company. He specifically urged the board to fill his seat with a Black candidate to help increase representation across the board. This representation, in turn, could shape Reddit's strategy in moving in a more inclusive and equitable direction. Ohanian made this decision in the midst of ongoing protests against police brutality after police officer Derek Chauvin murdered

George Floyd, a Black man, on camera. Ohanian understood that in the current political climate, what was not needed was another performative statement from a company lamenting violence against the Black community. In fact, his voice might not be needed at all in a time like this. Perhaps the very best thing he could do was hand over the very platform he built to amplify the voices of those who have been screaming to be heard. By believing that resignation could actually be an act of leadership, he understood the importance of constructing a more representative board, even if it meant forfeiting his own spot to create that space.

With my background in communications and as someone who is fascinated by human interaction, this action really stuck with me. I've come to understand that as a human being, when we develop a stance, it can be really hard to give it up. Simply put, it is natural that we enjoy feeling good. When we choose actions that do not feel good but have a net benefit, there is a level of wisdom and bravery that goes along with that. When Ohanian made this announcement, there was some online pushback labeling his choice as tokenizing. I define *tokenism* as a symbolic effort to be inclusive of overlooked populations that is largely appearance driven, and not truly indicative of systemic change. Although the tokenization of overlooked populations is unfortunately a commonplace corporate strategy, I don't believe that this particular example is one of tokenism. In Ohanian's case, it wasn't just that he prioritized increased representation on Reddit's board, it was that he intentionally created a transference of his resources, network, and platform to create an opportunity for his successor to have access to the platform he created. He wanted to ensure that whoever filled his seat would be equipped for success. It was about sharing his power and creating opportunity and access with individuals who want it, and not just puppet-eering someone because of their identity.

The impact of sharing one's power is immense, but it doesn't have to occur only when giving up one's seat—it can also look like passing the microphone, so to speak. I once had a leader notice my frustration during an executive meeting. Many executives were speaking over me and questioning my credi-bility. You may be familiar with the idea of *allyship*, a support-ive association of members of a marginalized or mistreated group. Well, what this well-respected leader did next took allyship a step further, and is exactly how I would describe *actionship*—when a person identifies an issue and takes action that results in positive impact. He interrupted the conversa-tion and reminded the other executives to actively listen to me. He did not paraphrase my message but instead reminded other executives that I was indeed a credible source and one who was owed their full attention and respect. This leader acknowledged his privilege and power. At that very moment, he also acknowledged the lack of respect and power dynamic that was taking place, and he counteracted it by sharing his power with me. I have never felt more seen or heard in a room where I was the "only." Being the only is lonely and frustrating, and it comes with constant pain. This leader didn't want praise for his actions; he wanted the folks in the room to give me their undivided attention and respect, and he used his power to demand as much.

So with this knowledge, what can we do next? I want to share a quick story with you that I believe is the founda-tion we must start with. Let me kick this off with a question:

What does true love look like to you? Television and movies will suggest true love is romantic but I think that true love is falling for someone whom you don't know, in a far deeper and nonromantic way. My brother works for the NFL and invited me to attend the 2022 Super Bowl where the Los Angeles Rams faced off with the Cincinnati Bengals. At the top of the game, a senior gentleman who was seated in front of me started to weep. Me, being the curious and human interaction–driven person that I am, decided to ask him why he was crying. He told me that he had been waiting for this moment his entire life. He had been a Bengals fan since he was a child and the team felt like his family, so to be able to use his financial resources to physically watch them get to the Super Bowl moved him to tears in an overwhelmingly meaningful moment.

This older gentleman had fallen in love with a team of people he had never met but only ever watched. Even as players joined and left the team through the decades, he loved the team unwaveringly and they occupied a meaningful place in his heart. How is it that we are able to fall in love with people we don't know? Well, with sports, the fanship and camaraderie are integral to the sport itself. We don't need to personally know these athletes in order to support them, hope for their success, and propel their growth. We love them without ever needing a conversation, without ever thinking about individual identities, just loving them simply because.

What if we could expand this idea beyond the sports arena? What if it were possible for us to love and support people we've never met? To just understand them in the most basic of contexts, stripping away race, age, gender, and all the other complexities that we fight over every day, but choosing love unwaveringly? When Russia invaded Ukraine in February 2022, terrified citizens hurriedly rushed to evacuate their homes as bombs and missiles started to drop and dismember cities. With the seriousnes of the invasion, women and children were prioritized for evacuation as able-bodied men remained to defend their country. I would be remiss, however, if I didn't address the horrifying footage that showed Black women and children being forced off trains in order to make room for white people and children, showing that even in the midst of life-or-death situations race still played a crucial factor. Polish mothers and citizens flocked to the train stations to leave their baby strollers and wheelchairs, something most of us would never think about in a situation of war. The captured photographs of empty strollers and wheelchairs awaiting the incoming trains of refugees who were able to escape are simultaneously heartbreaking and overwhelmingly moving. These photographs remind us that it is people who are on the other side of headlines. That there are families made up of teething babies, disgruntled toddlers, maturing teenagers, or sweet elderly grandparents who are fleeing for their lives, who shared tearful, gut-wrenching goodbyes with their loved ones and may never return to their home as they once knew it. These Polish citizens knew nothing about the occupants of these incoming trains besides the fact that their home country was under siege, and they still gave up their needed resources for those in more dire need. This is what I will argue DEI work is founded on. Fiercely loving someone you may never meet, but loving them all the same because they, too, are human. If we could allow this love to transcend all else, the world would look very different.

However, as we all know, we aren't there yet and the Great Divergence continues to persist. This doesn't mean we can't get there, but it does create our starting point. In order to build that unconditional love, we have to understand how similar we all are so we can start to give the love we hope to receive. We must take the time to really get to know each other, for through that process we will be able to find our common ground. Taking these steps will build our propensity for limbic cultivation until exercising this unconditional love becomes a natural muscle we are able to unconsciously flex. This translates directly into the workplace, because the workplace is composed of humans who all share universal human urges. Humans, as social creatures, want to feel connected. We want to feel fulfilled and motivated, to be valued and seen. Genuine rapport has to be built, and we need to understand the challenges that exist for us as individuals, both inside and outside of work, so that we can all show up to work as our full selves with our full capabilities. In order for organizations to really propel influence in DEI, they have to understand the fundamentals of human behavior and truly recognize what motivates others to care and want to drive impact.

To fully bridge the Great Divergence, we need to turn our gaze to the future. Yes, we *must* understand our history, and the full and unabridged history that shows us just how much darkness and suffering humans have been able to enact on each other, because it shows us what we are capable of and what we need to continually create a growing distance from. But we cannot forget that we owe so much more to our descendants than we do our ancestors. We continue to stand on the shoulders of giants, and one day that will come sooner than we care to admit we will be the shoulders on which others will stand, and we owe it to them to provide the foundation for a brighter and clearer future.

Chapter Reflection

As you read Chapter 1, what really resonated for you? What made you feel uncomfortable? What makes you hopeful? What is something you learned that you did not know before?

Activity: Decoding Human Behavior

How does one move from allyship to actionship? In order for organizations to propel influence in DEI, they have to, yes, understand the fundamentals of human behavior but first must recognize their ability to influence and determine outcomes. This starts on an individual level. Before *you* can influence your organization, you must first understand your own privilege and power, how you allow others access to that privilege and power, and plan your steps for action. Let's break this down.

Step 1: Assess Your Privilege   I define *privilege* as the unearned and mostly unacknowledged societal advantage that a restricted group of people has over another group. Most of us do not consider the many variables that affect the way we perceive others or the way others perceive us, which leads to more blind spots than we may realize in social or professional settings. For example, folks who grew up wealthy may not have a sense of how different life can be for those who did not. The same holds true for those who grew up as members of advantaged populations. To assess your privilege, write down all of the ways in which you identify. Then categorize your responses as "majority," meaning commonplace and generally accepted, or "minority," meaning less common or facing discrimination. As a best practice, ask each member of your organization to complete this exercise.

Identity Category (unearned identifiers)	How You Identify (your response)	Privilege Level (majority or minority)
Race and Ethnicity		
Gender		
Gender Expression		
Sexual Orientation		
National Origin		
Age		
Mental/Physical Ability		
Appearance		
Language Skills		
Education Level		
Family Background		
Political Beliefs		
Religion		

Step 2: Assess Your Power   Power is your ability to influence and determine outcomes. Although some privileges inherently come with power, power is also relational and can be earned. Think about your organizational role, your network, your voice, your platform, your access to opportunities. What control do you have over determining outcomes in your personal and professional life?

What level of influence do you have in your professional life to determine outcomes?	How does this give you opportunity to impact DEI work at your organization?
What is your organizational role? Do you manage a team? Do you have access to senior or executive leaders? Do you make decisions that affect your organization? What relationships are most beneficial to you? Do you have a platform? Do you have a professional following? In what ways do you give others recognition? When do you ask for others' opinions? Do you find growth opportunities for those who want them? Do you give others opportunities to present and speak on topics they're knowledgeable about? Are you part of interview panels? Do people come to you seeking advice?	

Step 3: Distribute Your Power and Commit to Actionship
Distributing your power means providing access to those who don't have it. It's Alexis Ohanian taking action to make room for his successor, it's Polish citizens sharing their resources with Ukrainian refugees, it's the leader who forced the men in the room to acknowledge my credibility as a Black woman in the DEI space. Distributing power positively and intentionally is actionship.

Write down three specific actions you are going to take to provide others access to your workplace power.

1. _____

2. _____

3. _____

2

Who Let the Dogs Out?

HI THERE, GLAD to see you made it to Chapter 2! Now that we have officially kicked things off, allow me to reintroduce myself. My name is Netta, and in this chapter, we're going to explore some of my biggest fears—dogs and company surveys. Okay, alright, I'm joking about the first one (I actually am terrified of most dogs but that's not the topic for this chapter), but we are going to dive in and unpack company surveys—what they are, how they are used, and how they can be used most effectively.

You Have the Right to Remain Dishonest

Company surveys are like your corporate Miranda Rights. Anything you say can and will be used against you in a court of workplace. Now for all of you folks who already have a prepared rebuttal, you know where to find me— on LinkedIn! But before you send that strongly worded message, hear me out for a second. Remember in Chapter 1 I said that this journey will require us to experience a level of vulnerability. There will be points throughout this book in which you feel challenged, and perhaps now is one of them. But most important, we will get through this together. I want to remind you that this book is not just about you—it's about building an inclusive organization that unequivocally includes you but also very much includes other people who may have completely opposite experiences and opinions, which is the beauty of inclusion. If you are an individual who hasn't had negative experiences with company surveys, I'm going to challenge you to place yourself in the shoes of other subsections of the population who have.

As is the case with most behaviors, responses are largely learned. Our bodies will encounter a situation, a physiological response will be triggered, and our bodies will inherently associate this situational response in the future. My fear of dogs wasn't something I was born with. I didn't come out of my mother's womb with a strong aversion to "man's best friend." This fear was something I had learned after being bitten by three different dogs on three separate occasions. And despite even needing stitches, it's also a fear I've really wanted to unlearn. When I was younger, my dad wanted to help me overcome this fear by getting me the sweetest little puppy. The puppy wanted nothing more than to play with me, but by that time I was already terrified and would run away every time it approached me. Needless to say, that puppy did not end up becoming my best friend. Fear of surveys, just like fear of dogs, is something people learn. When you've been bitten enough times, your body will start to sound the alarm each time you're in a similar situation as a cautionary and protective measure. Folks who have learned to be critical of company surveys have learned this for a reason. No one is born with an innate fear of questionnaires;

rather, they have been metaphorically bitten at some previous point in their lives.

Let me pose a question: Have you ever wanted to tell someone how you really felt, but were too afraid to because of the possible repercussions? Well, this is how many of us feel in the workplace, and it is an experience that is not unfamiliar for many systemically overlooked populations. Why might that be? Well, the answer partly lies in basic mathematics. Let's break it down: picture yourself on a team where you are the only person with a specific identity. Maybe you're the only woman, the only Black person, or LGBTQIA+ person, and so forth on your team. You haven't been having an amazing experience so far, and when the end of the year rolls around, you finally have a chance to tell it all in the annual company engagement survey. The survey is anonymous as is standard for company surveys. You don't submit your name or email and you start filling it out, providing honest feedback as to your various experiences. But once you reach the end of the survey and you're asked to provide your demographic information, you realize you've been entirely too honest and on top of that you are the only person on your team checking the box "Female," or "Black," or "LGBTQIA+." As you stare at these boxes, you realize that your answers will absolutely point back to you as there is no other teammate of yours who will also check these boxes. With that, the anonymous part of the survey is, well, not all that anonymous anymore.

This is my story. Time and time again, I have sat in front of my computer screen staring at surveys I know will offer me little anonymity, and I have to weigh out the pros and cons of freely expressing my genuine experiences. I know if I have had these experiences, it's probably not too farfetched to think that other folks have also had similar experiences, even those who aren't from systemically overlooked populations. Feeling fearful or apprehensive of completing company surveys is much more universal than we may realize. I really wanted to understand how people of all backgrounds and experiences feel when it comes time to provide feedback for their companies, so I decided to go directly to the source.

With over 100,000 followers on LinkedIn, I asked my audience their thoughts on company surveys and conducted a 24-hour poll to gauge how people generally feel. It was an interesting experiment that garnered nearly 2,000 responses. Roughly 59% of folks answered that they did not feel comfortable taking and answering company surveys honestly, and 41% of folks answered that they did. I also received nearly 100 comments from individuals who wanted to provide more insight into how they voted. The comments shared with me had three general trends: folks felt fully comfortable sharing their honest feedback with their employers, they absolutely did not feel comfortable sharing their honest feedback, or it largely depended on the company itself and needed to be taken on a case-by-case basis. The majority of the comments, however, echoed the poll itself—with individuals stating that they did not feel comfortable answering company surveys honestly with additional context. Reading through these responses, I was struck by the similarity of reasoning behind this reticence. Almost all of the comments that stated a discomfort with company surveys highlighted these three important reasons: lack of anonymity, potential for retribution, and a lack of follow-up from the company in response to identified issues.

Let's take a closer look at some of the comments folks shared. One person stated, "I absolutely [answer surveys honestly]. Then I got to the last three questions: 1. Gender: Female, 2. Race: Black, 3. Department: Cardiology. Gulp. Part of the problem with data collection is that there's no representation for some of us. I am the only Black and only Black female nurse practitioner in my department. . . . Zero hope for anonymity. They'll know exactly whose engagement survey that was." Another comment read "Speaking from personal lived experiences, I've witnessed a large organization give their department a poll and then use that data for personal vendettas. And there is no privacy if the organization can detect your IP address and match it with the time/date. In addition to polls, be aware of personality quizzes, like the MBTI or StrengthsFinder. They're rooted in racism, ableism, and eugenics." One person even countered my question with another thought-provoking one: "Does my employer feel comfortable with me telling my truth?" Do companies even want to know the honest truth about how their employees feel and will they act on their findings, or are they simply following a corporate standard?

Wherever you fall in this debate, what cannot be contested is that there is a significant portion of the workforce, and in some cases a majority, that does not find company surveys to be effective. If this is the case, why would we marry ourselves to an unproductive and time-consuming process? Why can't we design a new process that would actually enable us to get a truly accurate understanding of how employees are feeling about their organization, without any fear of retaliation? We've previously discussed the importance of decoding human behavior and how that will enable us to build authentic connections with one another. The next step is to begin decoding the workplace. We need to understand how people feel, think, and operate as part of an organization.

Decoding the Workplace

Before we jump into possible solutions, let's make sure we fully understand the problem at hand. Why do companies use surveys in the first place? Surveys are typically used to provide insight into how employees feel about company leadership, values, and so on. This can be helpful because one of the biggest costs for a company is the financial support it takes to interview, hire, and train new people and get them to a place of meaningful contribution. If companies extend their resources only to have substantial turnover, they will find themselves in a consistent financial deficit. One critical consideration companies must acknowledge is *who* the individuals are who are actually taking the survey, and not simply the responses they are receiving. Organizations need to take a step further and really understand their sample selection. For example, if an organization conducts an annual survey that finds that 95% of their organization feels satisfied, supported, and respected in the workplace, then that organization might give themselves a pat on the back and simply move on until the following year when the next annual survey is sent out. However, if the organization has 95% of its demographic identifying as part of an advantaged population, then the survey would do very little in uncovering the experiences of the 5% of employees who come from systemically overlooked backgrounds and who may

have had many more negative experiences than their coun-
terparts. If organizations simply assume that high percentages
of satisfaction equate to success without really understanding
the outliers, they have a strong chance of forfeiting insight
into the actual trends that are occurring with the organization,
and they could inadvertently perpetuate or even strengthen
the inequities that currently exist within their organization.
Going back to my LinkedIn poll, one person responded,

"I am comfortable completing the [company] survey,
but I don't believe the data is used to address legitimate
concerns. If the majority of the respondents completing
the surveys are satisfied with [the] company then the
minority respondents' concerns aren't addressed."

Simply put, majority satisfaction in a company that is not
representative does not equate to an effective and inclusive company.

Another challenge company surveys present is the method-
ology used to capture data. Operationalizing the data collection process requires that the process is broad enough to
act as a catch-all. But something we know is that one size
oftentimes does not fit all, and in this case, a generic list of
questions cannot capture the nuances and dynamics of the
unique challenges various organizations face at the specific
stages they find themselves in. One particular difficulty I
have experienced firsthand is that there is a level of rigidity
that comes with surveys that have not truly adapted the evolution of cultural practices. I will continue to argue that one
of the most fundamental elements of building an inclusive
organization is to fully address and respect the power of language. There are an immense number of cultural identities,

and these cultural identities remain in a state of constant evolution. Language is expansive, and through creating and expanding our vocabularies, we continue to bring new ideologies to life. This brings us back to limbic cultivation, a concept I introduced in Chapter 1. In order for us to start shifting our understanding, we need the tools that will enable us to do so. Language is an incredibly powerful tool that makes things real, and as any linguist will tell you, languages are alive and constantly shifting. We need to learn how to move in tandem and integrate these shifts into our processes, and we can do this by putting power in the hands of those who will use these words to create their own identity.

For example, we can start with one of the most basic demographic questions. Any variation of the question "How would you identify yourself?" will leave the reader faced with a series of checkboxes that may or may not encompass their identity. One concern that has been brought up to me time and time again is the limited groupings by which individuals are forced to identify but that do not give full weight to their cultural identity. I've learned that there is a population of Middle Easterners who do not identify as white, despite not receiving their own ethnic box to check. They are then left with the decision to check "White" or the other generic catch-all, "Other." Can you imagine the feeling of checking "Other"? There is so much erasure that is enacted by that one word. If you do not fit into any of the other prescribed buckets, you will be categorized as "Other" and become grouped with other individuals who may share very little cultural overlap with you. If that is the depth of identity a survey will explore, then we need to understand how the resulting data analysis will be skewed, because we will not be able to obtain a fully accurate analysis. This is why it is so important to understand the weight and implications of erasure when collecting data, and why we need to leverage language that will mitigate this from happening.

Now it's common practice for organizations to have their human resources (HR) team create surveys. Would this solve the issue of inflexible and generic language? Well, maybe it could solve that particular issue if the company were intentional with the survey language used but it would open up the organization to a whole other dilemma. First off, when these company surveys are created and conducted internally, the team that handles this responsibility is usually HR. Now this is not to take any sort of dig at HR—I have met incredible people in HR who do amazing work and are highly integral to company functions. But despite this, I have seen themes of misalignment between the HR team and the rest of the company. Through years of conversations I have come to determine that there can be a general feeling across employees that they cannot fully trust HR, because they feel HR's biggest prerogative is to support and protect the company and not individual employees. This notion creates gaps in what people feel comfortable openly sharing with HR, as again, people want to avoid a punitive recourse. However, this is a fully unfair burden to place on HR teams, and in my experience I have learned that even folks within HR feel afraid to openly share their thoughts. If HR personnel are also employees who are equally affected by the culture and processes within an organization, shouldn't they get a fair and equitable chance to share their experiences instead of being forced into the role of referee? Therefore, pushing this process onto internal employees will still not solve the issues about how company surveys are conducted and used.

Now that we've spent some time really delving into and identifying some of the challenges about company surveys, how can we begin to address these challenges and create new solutions that are able to sidestep these obstacles? Through my work as a leader in equity and inclusion, I have had the opportunity to establish a replacement of these company surveys with a new dynamic process that can address the specific needs of a particular organization and create a customized approach for the organization to take to disrupt some of the inequity trends that are taking place.

Dynamic Solutions for Dynamic Companies

In order for companies to create a truly anonymous and effective feedback process, they must outsource to third-party vendors who are able to ask targeted questions to address company-specific gaps and collect and transform the data into meaningful solutions the company can follow step-by-step. I've found this to be a highly productive strategy that can be tailored to each organization's unique needs. There are a number of third-party employee experience organizations that are tackling this well, but I'm going to share the approach I typically take.

When companies outsource to third-party vendors focused on employee experience, it creates a streamlined approach that promotes psychological safety and offers organizations top trends and tailored inclusive solutions for a deeper understanding of the various demographics that exist within the organization. It's no secret that one of the biggest joys of my work is the opportunity to really connect with and get to know the people I work with, so I like to kick off this process by leading a live session focused on building trust and credibility for people across the organization. I typically host one to four sessions depending on company size to give us multiple opportunities to get people acclimated and build rapport. After these sessions, I break the organization down into focus groups that will provide insight into company trends. I recommend these focus groups be as individualized as possible to ensure a sense of psychological safety. For smaller organizations, these focus groups are structured as one-on-ones to really give each employee the chance to build trust and rapport with myself. This setup allows people to elaborate and share details about their experiences, which is critical for a smaller organization that must retain employees in order to grow. For companies of larger size, I still re-create the individualized feel through leading virtual focus groups. In these larger sessions, participants are prevented from seeing who else is on the call so it feels like they are having an individual session. Together we'll walk through a deliberately calibrated list of questions that were formulated to be unbiased and uncover deep systemic trends based on existing company feedback. At the end of this chapter you will have the chance to view examples of some of the actual questions I use in this process.

Once I have collected the results from these questions, my team and I will then go through and analyze the data using a formula I created to understand the landscape of the organization in question. One thing to note is that this process correlates with the size of the company; larger companies will require a longer analysis period. Some of the topics explored in the analysis include workplace retention and experience, growth and development opportunities, psychological safety in the workplace, strategy, and perspective on company leadership. I also carefully examine the organization's current employee review process to identify any existing biases that could strongly affect an individual's perceived value or upward mobility within an organization. Once my team assesses the data, we are able to derive the organizational trends that need to be addressed and resolved.

The final step includes presenting these trends to the organization as a whole to provide transparency into the organization's current successes as well as the noted areas of improvement. Organizations that undergo this process must be committed to wanting to embed inclusivity into all of their operations and processes. I won't sugarcoat this—it will take financial backing and investment to incorporate these changes, but the organization must be supported by its board and executive leaders as it looks to refresh its policies and operations. However, this is just one action that is required. Organizations can change policies and operations all day, but if they have problematic employees and leaders who perpetuate a toxic workplace, they must remove these individuals in order to truly create an opportunity for structural change. These newly adapted policies must also include accountability measures and a clearly outlined plan of escalation in the event of any deviations from the policies. That way, there will always be an identified plan of action so employees know how to respond in the event that certain occurrences are outside the bounds of established protocol. Without both of these actions, organizations will be left chasing their tails, so to speak. Dog lovers—you know what I mean.

Now that the organizational trends have been identified, I provide each organization with a detailed plan that is tailored to its specific trends, as well as measurements and metrics that can be used to track growth and improvement throughout the year. By creating a holistic process, I am able to build trust with employees across an organization, collect meaningful and unbiased data, and create an inclusive solution that a company can follow step-by-step to track their improvements. Furthermore, employees are protected by an intermediary layer since organizations don't have access to individual answers, but rather get direct clarity into identified trends, as well as specialized and ongoing support in implementing solutions for their unique gaps. This ensures that all employees, regardless of level, role, or function, are able to participate with full honesty without any concern for retaliation.

Let me leave you all with a couple examples of how I was able to help companies of all sizes create solutions for gaps experienced by one of their employee demographics. After going through the process I've outlined, I was able to gain insight into the unique dynamics of each company in question. I provided each company with feedback on areas they were currently doing well in so they were aware of effective practices. I was also able to identify the needed areas of improvement. This first organization was a smaller startup and received feedback pertaining specifically to their LGBTQIA+ community. My findings demonstrated that the LGBTQIA+ populations within the organization did not feel like they had the health care support for their own unique needs. Through speaking with the employees on an individual basis, I came to the understanding that the LGBTQIA+ community wanted to have some financial support for gender-reaffirming surgery. This was a really important issue because they wanted to not only be able to identify as they choose but they also wanted the organization to put the financial resources in place to demonstrate that it fully respected and acknowledged their choice. By facilitating this process I was able to bring to light the particular needs of this employee demographic and devise a care plan with the organization to meet these needs.

The second organization was a larger enterprise, and their analysis found that the Black employee population across all departments and levels, as well as their employee resource group (ERG) members specifically wanted to gain guidance in shaping their career growth and navigating various workplace scenarios, as well as opportunities for advancement. They also wanted a punitive-free way to report aggressions. To solve these issues, I connected the organization with Dipper+, one of the internal tools I leverage within my company. Dipper+ is an application that specializes in providing ongoing career advice and tips for navigating workplace dynamics from the lens of an overlooked population and enables individuals to submit anonymous aggressions that can be thoughtfully shared back to their company. The Black employees at this second organization were able to use Dipper+ to connect with other professionals of color who had dealt with similar challenges and were in positions of power and could connect these employees to thoughtful, action-driven leaders, also known as sponsors, who could amplify their voices and provide them with leadership opportunities, ensuring that they had consistent access to pathways of growth.

There is so much substantial data that shows how employee happiness directly correlates to a company's growth and success. After all, if we are invigorated by the work we do and the people we work with and we all feel fully valued and respected, we are much more likely to enjoy our job and take pride in the work we do. Even though this process will require a concerted investment and commitment, it can absolutely transform an organization and unlock momentous potential for the organization to become an impactful and inclusive leader. We very much have the power to continue to shape our workplaces into equitable spaces in which we can all be heard and valued as our true selves. In Chapter 3, we'll discuss how to get past a fear of dogs. Only joking. We'll actually be exploring and breaking down the DEI framework I created based on my own personal and professional life experiences. See you there!

Chapter 2 Exercise: Driving DEI Impact by Establishing Accountability Through Action

In this exercise, I offer a framework for establishing accountability and success through taking action with a third party vendor. It is critical that organizations take appropriate steps to build trust with employees in order to get the feedback needed to provide transparency into current successes and areas of improvement. I encourage using this four-step exercise as a guide for improving understanding of your organization's current state so you can recognize organizational gaps and commit to dynamic solutions.

Step 1: Understand Your Influence and Identify Other Influencers

First things first, no matter how big or small a role, everyone holds a level of influence in an organization. You must think creatively about DEI solutions in order to engage and motivate others to do the same. You have the ability to drive DEI impact, and who you bring along on the ride will make or break your efforts.

Start with these considerations (write your responses next to each question):

What is your current role at your organization?	
Are you part of a team or working group? If so, what is the structure? Do you have direct reports? Whom do you report to? How do these individuals support you?	

Who can you rely on and shares the same motivations as you?	
Who are the people you are comfortable approaching with new ideas?	
Are others already committed to DEI efforts? If yes, then who? If no, then who are the stakeholders to bring on board who *would* champion these efforts?	
What team(s) do you need to engage in order to push these efforts forward?	
How will these efforts be recognized at a senior leadership level?	

Your responses should give you an access point on where to begin these conversations, who will amplify your efforts, and how to begin strategizing. Set up time to discuss your desire for greater accountability and create an action plan for next steps. Do not underestimate your own influence.

Step 2: Organizational Awareness and Employee Pulse Check

Now that you have support, it's time to gather concrete data so you can increase organizational awareness and understand employee sentiment. Doing so will enable you to identify gaps and prepare you for a successful engagement with a DEI practitioner.

The following is a list of statements to help you assess where you stand as an organization. Check "certain" if you are absolutely positive the statement is true, and check "not sure" if there is an ounce of doubt about whether or not the statement may be true. This simple assessment is the first step to building a layer of trust with employees because it will enable you to take action on uncovering gaps that exist.

Organizational Statements	Certain	Not Sure
100% of employees are comfortable taking company surveys.		
Leadership or a specified team tracks all employee demographic data without an "other"' checkbox.		
Employees are satisfied with their compensation.		
Employees believe they have a healthy work-life balance.		
Employees feel comfortable providing feedback about leadership.		
Employees feel their feedback is taken into consideration.		

Organizational Statements	Certain	Not Sure
Employees trust there will be action taken regarding feedback.		
Employees are comfortable providing honest feedback to leadership.		

This is not an exhaustive list, but the idea is that you cannot assume employee comfort levels or workplace satisfaction. If you checked "not sure" to any of the statements, I encourage you to take the next steps to engage a third-party vendor. Doing so will give your organization an opportunity to share that it has identified its own gaps and wants to hire a professional to foster a psychologically safe space, which in turn will make employees feel highly valued and build that layer of trust that you want to do right and make positive change.

Step 3: Preparing for Your Third-Party Vendor

Before engaging with a third-party vendor, it is imperative that organizations understand their gaps and demographic makeup and have predefined their budget, scope of work, and execution plan. Let's break this down.

Preparation Category	Example
Document Company Makeup	Percentage of employees by gender, race, ethnicity by team or level
Identify Key Gaps	High attrition, lack of diversity, rocky team dynamics, biased hiring practices, ineffective leadership, lack of trust

(Continued)

Preparation Category	Example
Outline Current DEI Efforts	Does the organization have existing DEI policies and strategies? Are there teams or individuals already focused on this work?
Determine Scope of Work	How long is the engagement? Is an organizational assessment involved? Are employee interviews needed? Will educational workshops or trainings be the focus? Does the organization need strategy and process implementation? Does organization need all of the above? Who will the vendor work closest with? Is coaching involved? Who is the target audience?
Set a Budget	Based on needs, define a DEI budget for the year. Financial planning is critical to ongoing success.
Execution Plan	How will results be executed? How will organization execute and continue DEI efforts? Who is responsible for accountability and program sustainability?

Step 4: Onboarding a Third-Party Vendor

Now that you've prepared for a third-party vendor, the next step is establishing trust between the vendor and the organization. Building trust starts with an organization's leadership team. Leadership should effectively communicate needs for a DEI vendor and allow employee input. When leadership acknowledges its own gaps and takes that step to hire a third party, employees feel a level of accountability taking place. Once a DEI vendor is hired, it's critical organizations make time (and room in the budget) for the vendor to host sessions and provide opportunities for people to acclimate and build rapport with the vendor. Then, employees will be comfortable sharing honest feedback and bring intentionality into DEI work.

Following is a checklist including all the steps necessary to ensure a successful and fruitful engagement with your third-party vendor:

- Gather employee demographic data.
- Identify major organizational gaps.
- Outline key goals of engagement.
- Establish a healthy budget for the year.
- Build trust with teams through communication and transparency.
- Define the internal influencers who will execute the plan.
- Outline the execution strategy.
- Hire a third-party vendor like Holistic Inclusion Consulting.
- Make space for vendor and employee connections.

3

Franchising the Framework

THERE ARE MOMENTS throughout our lives that we will one day look back on and say, "That was a moment that changed the course of my life." Sometimes we recognize it exactly as it's happening, and sometimes it takes us years to recognize. Either way, we depart from that moment utterly changed and facing a new north.

I had such a moment when I was in middle school. Growing up as the daughter of Liberian immigrants in suburban Rhode Island, it wasn't so much of an assumption as a fact that there weren't too many families around town that looked like mine. My hometown was a reasonably affluent and predominately white town. I loved my childhood, riding my bike down tree-lined streets with my best friend and exchanging family meals, swapping my mom's Liberian pepper soup with her mom's shepherd's pie.

But in tandem with these fond memories, I also had some trying ones. In eighth grade toward the end of a long school day while I was waiting to hop on the bus and head home, a little white boy singled me out in a sea of kids and said, "I heard that your family is from Africa. Let's see how far and fast you can climb up this tree." I was shocked. I'd never been spoken to like that directly, and I didn't know how to respond. My classmates stood around me, some of them snickering. It felt like they were jeering at me, waiting to see what I would do. Rage, anger, and fear bubbled up inside me, and all I wanted to do was shove that little white boy to the ground and tell him to take his mayonnaise-loving, unseasoned food–eating miserable excuse for a self back home to his mama who was sorry he was ever born. But I was too in shock, and instead I turned on my heel and walked away. It wasn't until I reached my front door that I finally succumbed to tears.

My mother greeted me at the door, and I shared the story with her through tears. She knelt down so that we were eye level. My mother wiped my cheeks and said in a firm but gentle voice, "I didn't bring you into this world to cry about it. I brought you into this world to create change." Then she grasped my hand and rose, taking me with her. It wasn't the little boy who shaped my life, though he definitely was the catalyst for the event. It was my mother who, in that moment and with those words, gave me the gift of bravery and power and helped set my course to my new north.

Finding Your North

I took my mother's words to heart and carried them with me every day forward. The following year when I started high school, I knew I wanted to make her words ring true. I decided that I was going to run for and win the office of class president. I was committed to this vision of school leadership, and I wouldn't let anything stop me. I never wanted to be made to feel as small as that boy made me feel back in eighth grade, and I wanted to do everything in my power to prevent other students from being made to feel small. I mobilized my friends, and we organized a campaign like my town had never seen. We walked our eighth-grade middle school halls holding signs reading "Vote for Netta, she'll make the high school better!" I knew once I entered ninth grade, which was the start of my high school experience, that I would enroll in honors courses, participate in mock trial, practice public speaking; I basically wanted to do everything I could to make sure that no one could say that I didn't outright earn my place. After weeks of campaigning, I finally did it: I was elected president of the freshman class. As I stood on the stage in our auditorium, beaming widely while shaking the student council teacher's hand, he looked me in the face and asked, "Are you ready for your big gig? You know the freshman class president gets to fold flowers on the float for the community parade." Shaking my head, I responded "No, I'm not here to fold flowers for the float; I'm here to create change." He laughed so vibrantly. I mean, it was so striking that I started to laugh, too. But, guess what? I did just what I told him that I'd do.

At my young age as an adolescent I realized that, like the late Dr. King, I too, had a dream. I dreamt that every student—regardless of race, class, gender, sexual orientation, ability, or any other discerning factor—would feel like a welcome and respected member of our high school community. I wanted to form a massive movement of everyone who had ever been made to feel "othered" or excluded and ensure that they knew they deserved to take up all the space in the world that they wanted to, that they mattered, and beyond that, their voices and experiences were *needed*. That's the thing about exclusion—it cuts the same regardless of the reasons behind it. Instead, we would stand up for each other, stand with each other, and learn to share our power so that we all would remain shrouded within our shared protection.

As I started to speak more about my experience as a young Black student, other students started to feel encouraged to speak out about their experiences and the ways in which they had been ostracized. As we started to share our stories and understand the overlapping themes, we realized that these stories needed to be shared. This led to a massive performance in my high school auditorium that showcased a series of skits that created a glimpse into our shared experiences. It was such a massive event that we even had news coverage of the performance! On that day as I looked around at my fellow classmates all swelling with pride I knew that nothing was too big or out of reach, as long as we could work together.

This was one of the biggest lessons I learned in my adolescence: to create something out of nothing with no prior blueprint or instruction, and through that process actually becoming the blueprint for future trailblazers. Now don't get me wrong—I definitely had moments when I felt scared at the thought of creating a movement like my school and state had never seen. But I also heard my mother's words echoing in my ear, and so if I was going to fail, I would fail spectacularly. But what I wasn't going to do was nothing. I learned that a strong facet of bravery was creativity.

Oftentimes those who are creating something new don't necessarily have access to the best resources, but they have a vision and determination. I saw this exemplified in my mother's actions.

When my mother immigrated to America from Liberia, she brought with her the grit and scrappiness she would need to ensure her family's survival. While she worked full-time as a nursing assistant, there were times in my life in which we didn't have the easiest time financially. Even though it never registered for me as a child, there were periods of time in which things were a bit tight, and she needed to figure out how to sustain our finances. So she got creative. She reached out to the Liberian community across Rhode Island and put together a food sale. Among her many skills and talents, my mom is an excellent cook. So when she got home from work and took off her scrubs, she would don an apron and start whipping together the most delicious Liberian meals that she would sell to the Liberian community. Though I and the rest of our community never knew of our financial struggles, what I did see was the hard work that she tackled head on to make sure she could put my sibling and I through school and provide us with every toy or school resource we needed. Not once did my mother complain; she just figured out what needed to be done and made it happen. Watching her navigate the world with such calm and collected fierceness taught me deeper lessons about bravery than any book or movie I could ever see. I learned that you can't be afraid of something just because you aren't sure of the way to get there. You simply need to figure it out, and that can require you to adapt creative strategies. Everything that exists in our world was at one point created. Before that point, it didn't exist.

Imagine how much bleaker and emptier our world would be if people were too paralyzed by fear to try and create something new. We must at the very least try; we owe ourselves that much.

Devising Our Own Solutions

Fast-forward to when I was a young professional entering the corporate workforce as a specialist in recruiting with a DEI lens. Gone were the days of floats and campaign signs, but the lessons I learned had only become more deeply ingrained. After majoring in communications with a focus in behavioral psychology, rhetoric, and leadership in college, I wanted to tackle the workplace and continue on my dream of creating equitable and inclusive spaces for folks of any background to achieve their own success. Something I noticed rather quickly in my career was a lack of understanding around what diversity, equity, inclusion actually was and how it should be implemented into the workforce. It was such a pervasive disconnect that my own manager didn't even have a firm grasp on what I was supposed to do. This lack of structure caused massive confusion for companies, even for DEI leaders themselves. There wasn't a proper framework for integrating DEI, and even if there were, there weren't unified metrics to properly measure and understand the impact of DEI efforts. Once again I found myself staring down a completely blank path, devoid of any instruction or design. Like my mother, I simply rolled up my sleeves and got to work.

One of the most common misconceptions about DEI that I encountered was the idea that DEI meant hiring a person simply based on their background. Much like the (inaccurate) criticisms for affirmative action, people believed that

DEI would equip underqualified folks to obtain roles they weren't capable of, and pass over actual "qualified" candidates. Obviously this isn't even close to true because DEI work is centered on inclusive and transformative leadership that looks beyond the bounds of individual roles and responsibilities and considers the ways in which each person and team plays a critical role in the company ecosystem.

I started to bucket the work I was doing into separate categories to address the major gaps I was seeing across the corporate workforce. I did this partly for those I was reporting to and those reporting to me, but to be completely honest I mostly did it for myself. I needed to fully understand the issues I was solving for before I started to devise an effective solution. I could see that companies of all sizes and across all industries were all dying for a blueprint—a way in which they could define and develop DEI initiatives as fully embedded objectives and indicators of the company's success. As I started to explore the challenges companies were experiencing, the framework started to take shape. After all, in order to understand something, you have to give it definition. And in order to start a movement, you have to disseminate knowledge. So as I share this framework I urge you to join in this movement and share what you learn so that leaders in all fields can use this knowledge to better the spaces they enter. As we work together to franchise this framework, we will be able to reimagine our workspaces to empower the people who reside within them.

The Three Ps

I named my DEI framework the Three Ps: people, practice, and product. This powerful triad describes the necessary actors that will supplement one another to streamline impactful long-term results that yield higher employee productivity, performance, employee peace, and organically increased organizational profit. The first P is for people, who are at the very heart and soul of DEI work. We cannot be successful in DEI work without engaging every individual person. People are organizations' greatest assets and should be their focus before all else. We can't even discuss practice or products if we don't have the people who will support them. A business can't operate if they don't have people to carry out each function. And a business also can't operate if there are people within the organization who are disinspiring those around them. A nourished, inclusive culture will attract collaborative, solution-oriented, and empathetic individuals who will be invested in cultivating a safe space for themselves and their colleagues. There are a number of ways to engage the people within an organization. The areas that I focus on are attraction and retention, employee resource groups (ERGs), and DEI programs.

It's not hard to tell when folks are being disingenuous, and the same thing rings true for organizations. People want to enjoy where they work and there has been substantial data that demonstrates that company culture can have just as big a draw, if not sometimes bigger, than compensation. Your mental health doesn't have a price tag on it, and if you feel truly miserable somewhere, the money can only keep you present for so long. Attracting people goes a step beyond recruitment because it incorporates inclusive and intentional practices throughout the recruitment process that would inspire potential hires to join the team. This can look like actively seeking out different conferences that support specific populations and networking with participating candidates to ensure diverse candidate pools. The notion that there are no capable people of color who can perform job functions is inherently racist and is more an indication of not developing pipelines from these populations into opportunities at the company. It can also look like highlighting some of the resources the company provides to support the needs of different employee groups to illustrate a level of thoughtfulness and awareness of creating a seamless work environment. For example, I've worked with companies that have created different supportive programs for veterans or veteran spouses who are re-entering the workforce or have held panels on financial programs to assist caregivers who are raising families or taking care of elderly loved ones.

Once an organization is able to attract these people, they need to have pathways in place to retain them. Companies must have thoughtful and individualized career paths for each of their employees to make sure that everyone is able to grow in the way that they want; otherwise, they would simply go to another company that offers that level of guidance and opportunity. I strongly encourage all managers to build genuine rapport with their direct reports and really understand how they can support their reports' career goals and trajectories. Managers should consistently meet with each of their direct reports to discuss career trajectories both internal and external to the organization. During these sessions, managers can help their reports uncover long-term goals and set up connections and resources that reports can use during their tenure at the company to help them grow in the way they want to. For example, if a direct report is interested in eventually managing people themselves, managers should provide leadership opportunities to help their reports get experience managing or mentoring new hires. If an individual is interested in learning more about another company vertical, their manager should connect them with leaders on that team so they can gain insight into the responsibilities and experiences of those working in that field. A good manager is first and foremost an advocate, and if a manager is not interested in helping their direct reports thrive and be successful, then they shouldn't be placed in a leadership or managerial role. Period. It's often said that people don't leave companies, they leave managers, and there's a strong reason for that saying. If a company is aware that a single individual has caused distress and flight for numerous other employees, then they are just as culpable by not removing that individual and choosing to sustain a toxic environment. Now, it's also important to note that companies should not wait to be alerted of toxic situations. There should be consistent monitoring of company culture through external third-party platforms as discussed in Chapter 2, as well as a focus on tracking the ratio of people leaving various teams and the demographics of those leaving, the duration folks typically work at the company, and which individuals are let go during company restructuring or layoffs. Numbers will tell a story, and companies need to be actively listening to what is being demonstrated to them. These are some of the accountability measures that should be put in place to evaluate effectiveness and take efforts to the next level. Leaders and employees who are simply not productively contributing or causing harm even after intervention need to be let go. There's just no other way around it. Inclusive succession planning is also critical and should be embedded in the onboarding stage.

Aside from addressing individual pathways, people need community spaces that intentionally foster equity and inclusion. This oftentimes takes shape as ERGs, strategic employee groups that span across different populations and lead programming, advocacy, business impact, and education for the different experiences and needs of the population they represent. It creates a way for people to embrace their full identities and connect with others who share those identities while welcoming actionists who want to understand more deeply and support the communities within the ERG. As a leader in the DEI space, I have created and improved established strategies for ERGs across organizations and institutions of all sizes. I recommend developing targeted strategies that embed DEI key performance indicators (KPIs) for each unique ERG to tackle. Leaders across each ERG should come together and determine the areas of focus for the group and should be paired with an executive leader to help conduct strategy sessions and amplify the work each group is doing. ERGs can also work together to create space for the intersectionalities between all communities, as we are all intertwined as humans and these intersectional spaces will increase advocacy, collaboration, and business alignment. For example, I oversaw the collaboration between a Middle Eastern ERG and an LGBTQIA+ ERG that invited journalists to discuss the deep fear, resistance, and pain inflicted on people who are part of the LGBTQIA+ community in the Middle East. These conversations are not always easy, but they are important and deserve to be highlighted as they very much affect peoples' lives.

DEI programming can also play an important role in supporting people within an organization. DEI programming is expansive and can be tailored to fit employee needs and interests. I have led DEI programs focused on creating equitable opportunities for folks from systematically overlooked backgrounds. Organizations need to examine existing societal gaps and recognize how these gaps can manifest within the organization. Simultaneously, organizations need to reflect on the power they do hold that can help counteract these gaps and create a more holistically equitable environment. One particular equity program I devised was during my time working with a tech company that leveraged its proprietary no-code software. We launched a program that would enable people from systematically overlooked backgrounds who were looking to pivot into the tech industry an opportunity to earn a full-time opportunity within the company. These individuals were mostly either self-taught technologists or graduated from coding bootcamps and had the opportunity to go through the company's technical platform training bootcamp. Should they successfully pass the bootcamp, they would then be guaranteed a full-time technical role at the company. Furthermore, all participants of this program were paid during the training period because they were dedicating at least 40 hours a week to learn the company platform. This company recognized that there was a lack of representation across their technical teams and enhanced existing trainings and programs to solve this problem. This company had only 500 employees but they took on the endeavor of a much larger company and were able to do so because they were creative and intentional with the program they established. I applied the same concept to intermanagerial programming for managers and direct reports to develop mentorship, sponsorship, and building respectful and collaborative cross-functional partnerships. The *people* part of the 3Ps framework emphasizes the need to meaningfully attract people to an organization, treat them right once they are there, and give them opportunities to grow so they can excel in their own pathways, so that in turn they will be more committed to positively affecting their organization.

The second P is for *practice*. Essentially this means to put your money where your mouth is. Effective DEI work is definitely not just lip service. We have seen how companies will jump on trends while they are "hot," like posting hashtags about Black Lives Matter, and yet in the same breath pour much of their wealth into institutions that maintain and exacerbate systems of violence against communities of color. In order for employers to succeed in transformative DEI work, they must be willing to put in the time and resources for intimate DEI learning and development for teams, implement DEI policies, and embed DEI education into company practice as early as the onboarding phases. The main components that make up practice are inclusive sustainability, policies that create thoughtful solutions to address employee needs, and inclusive learning and development education that is embedded from onboarding throughout employee tenure.

Inclusive sustainability can look different across industries, but companies that use a lot of tangible resources should have inclusive and equitable practices that drive environmental sustainability. The company can practice ethical thoughtfulness by diminishing the company's carbon footprint and investing in reusable materials. It could also look like emphasizing supplier diversity—thinking critically about the businesses the company partners with and choosing to direct company resources to businesses run by systematically overlooked owners or requesting an external vendor with which you want a person from a systemically overlooked group to lead efforts. I worked with a CEO who was very intentional about empowering vendors to increase representation and give folks opportunities to lead for their growth and advancement. This CEO's philosophy was if he was going to work with one of the Big 4 and couldn't find a MWBE (minority/women business enterprise) to do the work needed for the growth of his organization, then he was going to request that systemically overlooked people from the well-known accounting firm only send women or people of color to lead his project. He knew this would give folks the exposure to grow within their organization.

Now I want to pause here for a moment and outline that this is not tokenism; this is intentionality. The unfortunate reality is that not every person from a systematically over-looked background will have full access to opportunities, but this particular CEO took the strides to ensure that the people with whom he partnered would be holistically repre-sentative, whether top down or in terms of team overlooked demographics. This practice intentionally creates space for systemically overlooked populations to have direct opportu-nities and is a creative way to ensure this. In tandem with seeking out MWBEs, finance departments must actively track all vendors used by the company and should always consider opportunities in which MWBEs could be lever-aged instead. This is a very direct way to track quantifiable impact the company has been able to contribute to.

Company practices are also largely affected by policies. Some recurring themes these policies can address are mitigating microaggressions and creating accountability measures to prevent microaggressions from becoming commonplace within the culture. This can be incorporated as early as the interview process. Hiring teams should create unified interview questions that incorporate DEI values—such as adopting the term *culture add* as opposed to *culture fit*. A culture add is someone who may bring qualities or experiences that are not already present on the team, as opposed to finding someone who exemplifies the attributes already on the team. Specifically seeking out culture fits can lead to homogenous teams that can perpetuate exclusive practices that prevent the team from diversifying. Candidates who have a positive interview experience in which they are able to build rapport with their interviewers and get genuine insight into the company will be more likely to want to accept an offer should they receive one. I strongly recommend that companies provide opportunities for candidates to share their interview experiences, especially negative ones. If there is an interviewer at the company who is habitually committing microaggressions to the point of candidates losing interest in the company, then that's something leadership should be made aware of. In the event that this happens, the interviewer should be removed from interviewing responsibilities until they go through extensive scenario-based training that will equip them to conduct professional, empathetic, and inclusive interviews that provide an accurate portrayal of a candidate's abilities.

Practice can also mean retooling reimbursement policies. A company can offer to reimburse their employees, but it might not take into consideration that the employee doesn't comfortably have the ability to fund purchases or events with retroactive reimbursement, especially if the necessary procedures for reimbursement take time, which can place financial burden on an employee. Practice could also look like establishing DEI requirements for companies during acquisitions or partnerships, or providing flexible options for employees to work remotely or in office as suit individual needs. Practice means providing care stipends for employees who are going through gender transitions. It could mean covering childcare costs for employees. So many caregivers have to pay childcare in order to go to work. Think about the irony of that—instead of working to afford childcare, folks must pay childcare to afford to work. But the common thread within each of these practices is that they are directly supporting employee needs and take into consideration what people are actually asking for that would make it easier for them to do their jobs.

Practice could also look like integrating DEI into a company's business structure. One of my favorite bagel shops in Brooklyn, Nagle's Bagels, has it built into their business model that they will ensure a percentage of their positions to refugees, veterans, and people returning home from prison to help bridge the gaps that these populations face in trying to build a stable future for themselves and their families, and to build an employee base that is representative of the community the storefront resides in. I bet you never thought that eating a bagel could be radical but this is exactly my point—people can disrupt from anywhere at any time, they just need to be intentional with it.

The final P is product, and this is something I'm incredibly excited about as it's part of the new frontier of DEI work.

A lot of people don't know the impact DEI can have on directing financial growth. In fact, I have worked with numerous companies that have gotten multimillion-dollar contracts through the implementation of this framework, which has allowed them the ability to accurately measure the success from these initiatives and demonstrate them accordingly. Although many companies *say* that DEI is embedded into performance reviews, how exactly do they think they are tracking this if there isn't any sort of record or structure to do so? Well I got tired of side-eyeing these executives boasting empty words and went ahead and created a dynamic and detail-oriented software that captures the DEI work of every single employee in real time and incorporates automated reminders and transparent accountability. Now I feel your eyes getting watery and a virtual bear hug coming on, but before we hug it out, I want you to understand that if there isn't a concerted investment in an accountability product that tracks all employee efforts from bagel buying to pursuing inclusive health care resources, then a company's DEI efforts aren't real. Think about it. It's like saying we have a speed limit, but then having no consequences for speeding. It would be chaos and we'd see an increase of accidents and fatalities. Let's stop separating DEI from reality. DEI *is* reality because there are real people and real lives that are affected by how companies choose to execute decisions.

During my time working with a fintech software as service company, I was able to create an application that allowed the company to track and measure DEI impact by creating a streamlined and transparent way to unify employee-driven goals. This product is highly customizable and can be adapted to fit different team sizes and company needs.

I am currently working on taking this product to market so that all companies will have access to this technology. The application is actually quite simple in concept, but because nothing like it has ever existed or been shared wide scale, it's been able to solve some of the largest challenges within DEI—transparency, collaboration, and quantifiable impact. The application can integrate with different HR management systems to dynamically pull in each team across the company. Together, each team can select one of three DEI KPI pillars I have identified that each has a series of associated roles. As each team works on accomplishing their respective goals over the course of the year, they are able to track and view their team members' updates. Every employee can see what initiative each person is working on across each team, department, and pillar. In order for someone to successfully complete their responsibilities, they will have to submit information related to each responsibility. This will all be stored so that the impact of each employee is quantifiable and transparent for all to see and can easily be shared as part of the year-end review process.

This framework has helped revolutionize the embedding of DEI into everyday experiences in the workforce. It has created a guide that companies can follow and measurements that can be employed to illustrate impact and improvement with tried-and-true results. With consistency and executive support, the Three Ps are a highly effective solution that lays the foundation for other visionaries to plant their own seeds and sow their own ideas. After all, though this idea may have started with me, the last thing I would want is for it to end with me. So let's roll up our sleeves and get to work. There's a lot to be done, but it's not as scary if we do it together.

Chapter 3 Exercise: Join the Three Ps Franchise

It's time to take the Three Ps and apply them, analyze them, and make them yours. How well does your organization integrate DEI principles into its people, practices, and products?

Following are three charts outlining the Three Ps framework where each chart represents a different P. Use the space provided to analyze your organization's current efforts. Next to each category, write out the specific ways your organization is already practicing the Three Ps, the various ways your organization could be more inclusive in its current practices, the gaps or challenges that exist for you, and the gaps or challenges that exist for systematically overlooked people in your organization. (If you don't know what gaps exist, then write down what steps you're going to take to find out. How will you take action to understand what others are experiencing? How will you activate your power and privilege for actionship?)

People

What is your organization doing to attract new people and retain talent? Think about whether or not your organization has inclusive job descriptions, a standardized hiring process, gender representation, ethnic representation, flexible work-life balance, DEI onboarding resources, growth and development opportunities for employees, documented career pathways for growth, mental health resources, inclusive training for leaders, inclusive succession planning, fair and transparent salaries, safe spaces for underrepresented groups, team-building opportunities for teams, spaces to share about societal challenges, opportunities to drive community impact, mentorship and sponsorship programs, career development opportunities, or wellness programs. Are employees aware of the disparities that exist across gender, race, ethnicity, sexual orientation, and different lived experiences? What types of DEI-focused programs are being offered? Why would someone want to join your organization and what will make them stay?

People Emphasizes attraction and retention, growth and development, resources and community, psychological safety, mental and physical wellness			
What your organization offers	Inclusive practices you would like to see	Gaps or challenges that exist for you and why	Gaps for systematically overlooked people in your organization

Practice

Organizations love to talk the talk, but do they walk the walk? Practice is about putting in time and resources for DEI initiatives and education so employees have greater awareness, better access, and stronger capability to drive business impact. Practice represents DEI policies, education, and directives that make DEI efforts tangible. What inclusive policies does your organization have in place? Are there policies to address aggressions, also known as micro-aggressive behavior? What education is implemented from the onboarding phase for new employees to be part of your organization's DEI journey? How are DEI goals communicated and acted on? What inclusive policies does your organization offer? Is your organization intentional about establishing DEI requirements during acquisitions or partnerships or focusing on supplier diversity? Consider inclusive health benefits for caregivers, veterans, and transgender employees; tuition or student loan reimbursement; time-off policies as they pertain to mental health and wellness; policies to lessen carbon footprints; investments in reusable materials. How can you retool or embed various policies to ensure no one is overlooked?

Practice			
Emphasizes inclusive policies, DEI learning and development education, intentionality in supplier diversity, and overall inclusive business practices			
What your organization offers	Inclusive practices you would like to see	Gaps or challenges that exist for you and why	Gaps for systematically overlooked people in your organization

Product

Product is the way you measure your organization's DEI impact. In your role, what are ways that you are assessing the gaps in your own products or services? Are there disparities that exist? Has your organization found an impactful way to measure gaps and growth? If yes, is your process scalable? If not, how would you go about measuring success? If you had the power to ensure every employee within your organization had DEI impact top of mind, what would you do? How will you take this a step further by implementing a DEI product? Keeping DEI top of mind simply is not enough if the impact is not being measured.

Product			
Emphasizes integrating DEI with your organization's product, services, or platform in order to achieve greater financial growth and more inclusive innovation			
Products, goods, services, solutions, platforms your organization offers	Ways you are assessing gaps in your product or service	Ways to make your product more inclusive	Action steps you need to take

4

The Most Underrated Leader

LET ME TELL you a really exciting and completely fake story. You're sitting on a plane, munching pretzels and sipping your drink of choice, just minding your own business. You're ready to take a nap when suddenly you feel a hard jolt that shakes you wide awake as a strong wave of turbulence hits. You look for the flight attendant hoping for reassurance— they deal with turbulence every day—but instead you find a group of attendants huddled anxiously together. One of them tries to sound reassuring while yelling over the growing frantic cries of the passengers, but another loses their nerve and starts crying, "Our captain has never flown a plane—he has no idea what he's doing!" Chaos ensues as passengers become hysterical. The airline let him fly the plane because he *said* he was a FREAKING CLOUD ENTHUSIAST!

Alright, let's take a quick breath here so we can all get our blood pressure back down. Clearly this is a fictitious story; I'm not trying to traumatize any of my readers. But I am trying to make a point. An airline would never allow a completely inexperienced person with no prior knowledge or training to pilot a plane, even if they were indeed a self-proclaimed cloud enthusiast. Why? Because a person of this background has a very high chance of literally driving the plane into the ground. So if you wouldn't let a passionate albeit inept person be responsible for an aircraft, why would you allow it for a company? DEI, just like piloting an airplane, is life or death because DEI is inherently focused on seeing people as people and providing the support and direction needed to enable all individuals to have an equitable opportunity to achieve success in the workplace. When people are not seen as their full selves and do not receive the appropriate support, it can have massive detrimental repercussions, especially for mental health, that unfortunately could be deadly. Also, because DEI leaders are often people of color, this situation illustrates an additional way in which systematically overlooked populations are taken advantage of and forced to endure surviving topical agendas that don't actually improve their professional experience. Organizations are responsible for not only finding the right candidate with the proper skill set and background but also setting them up for success so that they can best support the organization's employees. Without this, we will see people leave the DEI space with potential post-traumatic stress syndrome based on the level and stress and trauma they encountered while working within this space. In this chapter we are going to explore the ways in which companies can set up their DEI efforts for success, from navigating the interview process for DEI candidates to actual onboarding procedures and establishing practices that enable a DEI team to be sustainable, effective, and impactful.

So take a second and ask yourself—what are you doing right now as an organization to set up your people to succeed and thrive? Or are you sitting back and watching people fail?

The Dos and the Don'ts

As DEI begins to occupy a more prominent place in organizational practices and policies, there needs to be uniform understandings of the requirements for searching for a DEI leader. I named this chapter "The Most Underrated Leader" because DEI is still a growing field and one that is not always awarded the full support and understanding required for any sort of measurable impact, despite playing an integral role across all departments. Effective DEI work is entirely people-driven and will require expertise in navigating cognitive, perceptual, social processes, and behaviors. With my background in communications and behavioral psychology and leadership, I see every day how my background has been a critical component in the ways in which I interact with people and how I'm able to navigate the different situations I encounter. During my time in college, I focused heavily on rhetoric and the criticality of messaging. Learning how to articulate feedback is an incredibly valuable skill, especially in DEI, because a poorly delivered suggestion can easily shut a person down and dissuade them from feeling comfortable enough for self-reflection and accountability, the first stages of creating improvement. Through my studies and training, I've been able to learn how to help guide people to a mental place where they feel safe enough to open up and identify the ways in which they can take the necessary actionable steps to continue to develop their inclusive and equitable efforts.

The First Don't

I want to start off by addressing a couple major misconceptions about working within DEI. Although it's not far-fetched to imagine that many of the individuals you meet who work in the DEI space are quite passionate about their work, passion is not the sole prerequisite to being an effective DEI leader. As is the case with any department in any company, DEI work requires a particular skill set that is built through field-specific training, experiences, and capabilities. It cannot be simplified down to a mere passion project.

My background in communications and behavioral psychology has also pushed me to reflect this work within my own life. I'm very conscious of my own mental state and consistently monitor my mental health so that I can be proactive in ensuring my own mental safety, which is fundamental to my ability to sustain in this work and be able to help other people on their respectful journeys. It also helps me approach challenging situations with a higher level of empathy and understanding so that I can meet people where they are at and help them get to the place I need them to be in order to be a productive force within the organization. Traversing these different scenarios and personalities is not an easy feat, and it definitely requires training and experience. However, communications and behavioral psychology are not the only areas of practice that would lend themselves to supporting an effective DEI leader. Any individuals who have a background in race relations, sociology, or behavioral research would also have had the proper training needed to handle the responsibilities of DEI leadership. Furthermore, people who are creatively solution-oriented, assertive, optimistic, empathetic leaders with an ability to take strategic risks would have the personality traits to weather the challenges of working in DEI. My ability to think about the misalignments cross functionally and craft solutions that can improve the current processes is a critical component. This is how I exemplify some of the personality traits that help a leader be effective in DEI. It's easy to become disillusioned, but the ability to continue pushing and remain optimistic is crucial to the longevity of this work.

Side-stepping these requirements while developing a DEI vertical in an organization will lead to individuals who are ill-suited for the responsibilities of the work and will likely be unable to drive sustainable and meaningful impact. A company wouldn't appoint a CEO simply because a person was interested in becoming CEO—they would have an extensive process in which references were checked and candidates would have to demonstrate their experiences and strategies for substantial leadership. The exact same needs to be done for a candidate in DEI—why would a company go to the trouble of hiring someone who isn't legitimately set up to drive organizational impact?

The Second Don't

Another misconception is that DEI is not essential to an organization the way other verticals such as finance or accounting are and doesn't require the same level of executive buy-in. People don't always understand how a lack of embedded company-wide DEI efforts can actually be a financial detriment for an organization. Furthermore, tokenism is not a successful demonstration of establishing DEI within a company. What companies should absolutely *not* do is grab the first Black person or person of color they see and appoint them a DEI role and then give themselves a pat on the back (that's a big yikes from me). At the same time, however, it is important to consider representation when building out DEI teams, which includes representation of all populations. We'll explore each of these misconceptions a bit further so that we can instead replace them with actions organizations *should* follow in implementing and integrating DEI. So let's go ahead and dive in.

Let me share a quick story with you all. I had a client who reached out to me because their organization moved them from their HR role to a newly created head of DEI position following the murder of George Floyd. They also happened to be the only Black person at the company. It was very clear to me from our initial conversation that they had not received any level of adequate support or training from their company, and they were also given an ambiguous title without job description, metrics, or direction. Furthermore, because this individual had come from the HR team, there was also a level of mistrust they would have to navigate, as we discussed in Chapter 2. This performative act on the company's part did little but ensure that this individual would have serious roadblocks in any efforts they made to drive impact. This could lead to another serious challenge of ad hoc organizational DEI efforts—burnout. As I mentioned, a large part of my effectiveness comes from my ability to understand and address my own needs. Individuals who are thrust into these spaces are often unsupported and undirected, as this particular person was. This can create huge amounts of toxicity and stress for these individuals as they try to navigate incredibly challenging work.

Now on the flip side, I've also seen individuals empower their entrance into DEI work. I previously worked with someone who was given the opportunity to join the DEI team at their company. This individual had previously spent years working in nonprofits that supported justice-involved populations. They had led an employment program for young men coming home from prison to help them gain meaningful employment opportunities while also connecting them to education and mental health services. They also worked with children dealing with parental incarceration to gain a holistic understanding of the challenges these populations faced on both the preventative and rehabilitative sides. Through this work they were able to more intimately understand the systemic barriers and pipelines that intentionally target so many communities and create massive inequities that affect education, employment, health care, housing, and so on (this list is nonexhaustive). They decided to pivot from law school into a career in tech because they wanted to build scalable and sustainable solutions that were designed for overlooked populations. Working within inclusion and equity was a clear passion for them, so when the opportunity to formally join their organization's DEI team presented itself, this individual was already strongly familiarized with the responsibilities and challenges of this work and could accept the offer with both eyes wide open. They were then able to bring their technical expertise to play an instrumental role in executing the initiatives set by the organization's vice president (VP) of Inclusion by building applications that could quantify DEI impact and use that data to direct future initiatives.

Constructing Your DEI Department

Before we dive into developing a DEI department, let's take a moment to establish what the reporting structure for this role is. I define a DEI leader as someone with the title of VP, senior vice president (SVP) or chief to demonstrate to the company that they are a senior leader within their own vertical. They should also report directly to the CEO or COO. This will enable them to interface with the top leaders at the organization and have the support and advocacy of decision-makers who can propel their agenda forward. It also creates guidelines to their salary band and level of responsibilities. Simply saying someone is head of DEI is too ambiguous and doesn't hold the necessary weight needed for this type of leadership and creates *major* pay gaps, which is systemic and widespread.

I also recommend that for organizations of up to 1,000 employees, there should be at minimum three full-time individuals on the DEI team. For organizations larger than 1,000 people, I recommend there being at least half as many people on DEI as there are on the HR team. This will enable the VP/SVP/chief of inclusion to focus on remaining strategy driven, the same way other VPs/SVPs/chiefs do. If the top DEI leader is too busy developing content and working on some of the more nitty-gritty pieces, then they won't be able to establish long-term goals. It is critical (and equitable) that the leader of the DEI department be given the same support in delegating their strategies to their direct reports to execute. Anything less and they will be unfairly unable to produce at the level they should.

Furthermore, as is the case with all other departments, DEI also needs to have an allocated budget and headcount for the roles that fall within the vertical. DEI should encompass all learning and development training because career pathing must inherently be inclusive and requires an intimate understanding of how individuals at the company want to grow. Learning and development will look different for individual contributors, managers, and senior leadership, as well as from department to department, so this can easily be enough for one person's full-time job. There should also be a fully dedicated DEI program manager. They would be responsible for supporting and guiding all ERGs as well as developing internal and external programs that will help retain and develop employees. There should also be a DEI technical analyst who can focus on analyzing trends about DEI and can help paint a picture of the effectiveness of ongoing programs and policies. They could track trends about hiring such as how far candidates make it through the interview process and if there are notable patterns in the interview phases that people of certain demographics make it through to. They could also monitor the typical duration that employees stay at the company to see if there are trends in the length a certain population typically works at the company and in what departments or levels the company sees the most flight. They would also be able to monitor succession planning to understand the company's ability to create smooth transitions. All this is to say that there is a ton of work that falls under DEI and that absolutely requires a trained and full-time team.

Selecting Your Candidate

When interviewing for a DEI leader, you want to really consider the personality attributes this person possesses. After all, they will be the one driving potentially challenging conversations and you want to ensure they can do so with compassion, empathy, and a clear solution-oriented focus. I recommend focusing heavily on behavioral questions that are largely open-ended. This will provide insight into how they approach different situations, and their strategy will also illustrate their previous experience navigating this role and their potential ability to jump right in and take the lead. After all, as DEI is a newer area of focus for organizations, there typically aren't too many predetermined processes on the organizations' sides; they are more so looking to the DEI leader to help guide these solutions.

I typically prefer practical questions that directly relate to job responsibilities. One question I recommend asking is, "If you were to join a 100-person organization, what are the first actionable steps you would take and how would your approach change for a larger organization?" This question will enable the candidate to demonstrate their knowledge of the interpersonal skills needed for this role. I will walk you through my suggested guide to their first 90 days momentarily, but in asking this question you want to see if the individual will be proactive in developing individual relationships with each employee. A 100-person organization is not too large that this DEI leader could not establish a plan to connect with each individual over their first few months in one-on-one sessions. Simply establishing an open-door policy or office hours isn't enough; the DEI leader needs to take initiative in speaking directly with each employee to gain a fundamental understanding of what the employees currently know about DEI, how they feel about DEI, how they see DEI embedded in their role, and the impact they wish to make on an organizational level in terms of DEI. This will be the DEI leader's starting spot—creating a unified understanding of DEI work and what it is, as well as truly understanding the motivations employees have so they can create strategies that enable employees to accomplish their goals in tandem.

Another question I recommend asking is, "What support would you need from the organization in order to excel in your role?" How the candidate answers this question will demonstrate how much they have thought about integrating DEI across the entire organization. How would they like executives to support DEI efforts to ensure accountability across the board? Do they mention having a budget that will enable them to add team members who can take ownership of different areas within DEI, leaving them to focus on larger long-term strategy and working closely with company leadership? Do they have a vision to expand on the resources DEI offers and collaborate with leaders in other verticals? These sorts of experiential behavioral questions will help illustrate the individual's ability to effectively step into their role and execute a tailored and well-constructed strategy.

The First 90 Days

So now after the interview process, you've selected a candidate you feel strongly about. Although they should have an idea of how they want to get started, I have some additional suggestions I recommend the organization think about to help create a smooth and streamlined onboarding process. The organization should introduce this person by having a company-wide fireside chat conducted by the CEO.

This will establish a legitimacy to the work the individual will be doing, as well as demonstrate the executive support they will have in rolling out and implementing strategies. During this fireside chat, the DEI leader should introduce themselves to the company and share that they will hold a company-wide meeting to describe their background and provide an agenda on upcoming DEI objectives and goals. It's important to have a high level of transparency so each employee can be aligned and aware of the tactics the company will employ to further develop their DEI efforts. This can include re-creating policies to be more inclusive and reflective of employee needs, adding and standardizing a DEI focus to interviews, actively tracking managers who are doing an exceptional job advocating for their direct reports' growth, or holding consistent town halls to provide a platform for employees to provide feedback.

During this company-wide introduction, the DEI leader will start to build trust with their new colleagues. Trust building is a critical component, especially within DEI work. Psychological safety is the cornerstone of effective DEI work and therefore the DEI leader must create that level of trust so that employees can become comfortable practicing the vulnerability and risk necessary to drive impact. This company-wide introduction is the perfect place for the DEI leader to share their personal reasons for joining DEI efforts. By demonstrating their own level of vulnerability, they will be able to set the tone for future conversations as well. They can also share with the company their upcoming plan of conducting focus groups and one-on-one conversations to assess the current understanding and implementation of DEI into company practices.

Some questions the DEI leader can pose to the company during this introduction to be discussed in on-on-one meetings include the following:

- What do you know about DEI, and what don't you understand about this work?
- What is your official title and job responsibilities?
- How is DEI work currently embedded in your role, and if you don't feel it is, how would you like to see it embedded?
- What excites you most about your role?
- How do you think DEI can positively affect the work you do?
- Which organization leader do you feel is currently exhibiting a strong dedication to DEI and how so?

These questions can help the DEI leader formulate an understanding of where they need to begin. It will enable them to understand each person and their motivations so that DEI can intentionally support these motivations. It will also point the DEI leader toward folks who have already started to incorporate effective and impactful practices and help amplify their work as well acknowledge their initiative. When possible, a DEI leader should try to meet with folks individually, but in the event of working for a large organization, they can also conduct smaller focus groups to still build that comprehensive understanding. DEI is a vertical that relies on trust, so each of these actions are meant to help establish just that. The first 90 days should be focused on executing an organizational assessment and building personal relationships with all employees. Building these relationships takes time and can potentially require some support, especially for an organization of more than 100 people. The DEI leader will need someone to assist in taking notes, assessing data, and creating trend analysis reports. There will be a lot of insights to cover and it is definitely not a one-person job, so I suggest organizations think about other leaders they could loop in to support this process, such as the CFO, SVP of general counsel, or VP of engineering. Once this organization assessment is completed, it will be able to help the DEI leader build momentum by having a thorough understanding of the company, as well as the dynamics that exist within it.

Successfully embedded DEI requires innovative leaders who are equipped to creatively drive improvement in this space, but it also requires organizational support. When organizations understand the impact that a concerted focus on DEI can have, and align their resources accordingly, then they will equip their DEI team for success. But if organizations are unwilling to place the same level of importance and support in DEI that they are doing for their other departments, then it's quite likely that there will be little improvement, and quite possible that any workplace toxicity and inequity will be magnified. So let's make sure that we take the time to find the right people to lead, compensate them properly, and provide them with the tools and support they need to be effective, lest we all end up metaphorically crashing and burning together.

Chapter 4 Exercise: Is Your Organization Ready to Hire a DEI Leader?

Let's play a game of 20 questions. If you think your organization has what it takes to hire a DEI leader (defined as a VP/SVP or chief-level position), then you are ready to play. Following is a grid of yes-or-no questions. You score one point for every *yes* you can honestly check, and you score zero points for checking *no*.

1. Does your organization have a goal of embarking on its DEI journey or expanding its DEI impact?	☐ Yes	☐ No
2. Is every senior-level leader (C-suite or equivalent) prepared to support company-wide DEI initiatives?	☐ Yes	☐ No
3. Is your organization committed to ensuring every single employee takes part in driving sustainable DEI impact?	☐ Yes	☐ No
4. Is the organization prepared to re-create existing policies or implement new ones to be more inclusive and reflective of employee needs (e.g., adding a DEI focus to interview standardization, embedding DEI into employee performance evaluations, revisiting HR policies and benefits, offering more employee resources)?	☐ Yes	☐ No
5. Will a prospective DEI leader be a senior leader within their own vertical with a VP, SVP, or chief title?	☐ Yes	☐ No

6. Does your organization have an allocated budget for a senior-level DEI leader equivalent to budgets of other VP/SVP roles (or roles of the same level)? ☐ Yes   ☐ No

7. Would the prospective DEI leader report to the COO or CEO and not to the HR leader or CPO? ☐ Yes   ☐ No

8. Does the prospective DEI department have an allocated budget and headcount for expansion of the team, external partnerships, technical platforms, and learning and development resources? ☐ Yes   ☐ No

9. Have leaders identified the organization's shortcomings as they pertain to DEI and can leaders speak specifically to the organization's targeted growth areas? ☐ Yes   ☐ No

10. Do leaders have an onboarding action plan for the prospective DEI expert to share during the interview process? ☐ Yes   ☐ No

11. Are leaders able to exemplify the level of support a prospective DEI leader will have on joining the organization? ☐ Yes   ☐ No

12. Are leaders able to demonstrate what steps they can take to advocate for the implementation of a DEI road map? ☐ Yes   ☐ No

13. Can the company commit to embedding DEI accountability measures for employees by allocating funding toward a DEI measuring tool? ☐ Yes   ☐ No

14. Have leaders identified which skill sets, experiences, and behavioral-based interview questions will be most important to assess? ☐ Yes   ☐ No

15. Can leaders speak to the autonomy and opportunities this DEI leader will have to develop and implement their own strategies? ☐ Yes   ☐ No

16. Is the CEO committed to supporting this role through amplifying messaging, increasing awareness, and promoting advocacy on a monthly basis? ☐ Yes   ☐ No

17. Is your organization prepared to undergo an extensive and honest organizational assessment? ☐ Yes   ☐ No

18. Is the organization ready to pivot and adopt a flexible, sustainable DEI program? ☐ Yes   ☐ No

19. Does your organization have a 90-day plan for the prospective DEI leader? ☐ Yes   ☐ No

20. If only hiring one member for the DEI team, will there be other employees to assist in taking notes, assessing data, and creating trend analysis reports? ☐ Yes   ☐ No

Count your points (1 yes = 1 point)   **Total Points**

If you scored 20 points, congratulations, your organization is ready to take that big first step in hiring a DEI leader. If you scored less than 20, then before you can craft that exciting job description, before you can ask for those references, your organization should reflect on the nos in order to prepare for the success of your DEI leader.

5

Sustainable Learning

Upgrading Your Learning and Development—MapQuest Directions to Google Maps

LONG, LONG AGO when dinosaurs used to roam the Earth, we humans had only one trustworthy source of navigation to get from point A to point B: MapQuest. Okay maybe I'm exaggerating just a little bit; it was at least a few millennia after dinosaurs, but either way, without these preprinted static directions, our species would be almost at a complete loss in finding our way. It was during this time period that I took a road trip with a close friend of mine from Boston to Quebec, Canada. Now for those of you who predate MapQuest, imagine a website where you could enter your starting point and destination and it would output a series of directions you would need to print out and bring with you on your travels, while you simultaneously send a quick prayer that the streets and highways listed were correct and still even existed. During this seven-hour road trip into Canada, somewhere my friend and I made a wrong turn. Quite honestly, it's possible we made a few wrong turns, but with nothing but a preprinted set of directions, we were a bit up the proverbial creek without a paddle. Luckily we made it into Canada, but were not sure how to get to our final destination in Quebec. After a few hours of confused circling, we were able to flag down some nice Canadians who we hoped could help us right our course. Unfortunately, we were in the French-speaking province of Canada, and as two English speakers, we found ourselves at a bit of an impasse. Finally, after a few attempts we were able to find a gentleman who spoke enough English to help us get back on track and successfully reach our destination. To this day I remain grateful to this man who was able to guide us from a place of misdirection into a place of understanding. Now for this chapter, I will finally pay forward that act of kindness and act as your guide in this journey of sustainable learning. Luckily, we have some better tools today that we didn't have all those years ago (thank you, Google Maps) that are able to move more dynamically with us and course correct in live time, instead of relying on the kindness of strangers. So let's dive in and explore the importance of sustainable learning and the navigational challenges one will face without a proper dynamic road map.

I once worked with a company with an individual who was great at his role. He possessed all of the expert technical capabilities needed to excel in his position. Those who had the opportunity to work with him admired and appreciated his work. However, in tandem with his excellent technical skill set, he possessed some less attractive personal qualities: he was arrogant and condescending to those around him. Unfortunately (or fortunately for him), he was related to one of the founders of the company and found himself protected by nepotism. As the company began to grow and his vertical needed more people, he was promoted to manager and began leading a team. Even though he had much to share with respect to the role itself, he left much to be desired as a manager responsible for others' success and development. His behavior was overlooked in lieu of his performance until it became a potential lawsuit for the company. Most of the employees affected by his behavior were women and people of color, and with mounting evidence and a lack of response from the organization, it got to a point where the company could no longer afford to ignore all of the complaints they were receiving. Not having standardized and concerted growth strategies available to all employees creates deeper bias and systemic gaps in the organization that will ultimately cost the organization a tremendous amount of money as they struggle to retain strong talent and need to keep up with the costs of hiring and onboarding short-lived employees. Now I'm not advocating for creating space for people who are toxic to those around them, but I do think that individuals possess certain strengths that can make them beneficial to organizations if they are placed in the proper space with the proper responsibilities. That is why career mapping is an integral part of an organization's success, sustainability, and longevity. For those of you who may be unfamiliar with the term, *career mapping* is the thoughtfully constructed pathway of growth for an employee. It includes having a solidified plan with identified goals that an employee can meet in order to develop and ascend within an organization. Career mapping should include a consideration of the individual's interests and goals to ensure that each employee can work toward a future that they are actively interested in and motivated by. When organizations do not have inclusive and identified career mapping plans, whether it's because they lack preparation or are quite frankly uninterested in providing them, people are unable to grow in the ways they want.

Becoming a manager is just *one* way for someone to grow within their role; there are also other ways in which someone can become even more of an expert in their field without having to shift their duties to having to mentor and guide less senior individuals, especially if they are ill-equipped or uninterested in doing so. Having a lackluster manager oftentimes enables poor management practices to trickle down the vertical and have rippling repercussions. Unfortunately, without any other plan of action, this seemingly natural progression ends up having a costly impact in more ways than one. Going back to my story, although this individual was great at their job functions, they did not have the aptitude or interest in becoming a manager. There were repeated situations in which this person's direct reports complained about inequitable treatment, exclusive behavior and language, and a lack of advocacy from their manager. This resulted in high turnover on this particular team, and it became a stressful situation where employees saw time and time again that the company did not respond to individual complaints. Finally, after enough people spoke up, the organization had no choice but to let the individual go, because a lawsuit would be even more costly than high turnover in terms of money, time, and reputation. This lack of preparation and career mapping ended up costing the organization multiple employees who were all great at their jobs but not adequately supported in their respective needs. Had there been a well-thought-out plan, the organization could have potentially retained all of the employees, provided an opportunity for the individual to continue to develop their expertise and guide the overall department, and hired someone more interested and better suited to management to carry out that role.

The Oprah of Programming: Everyone Gets Learning and Development!

In order for organizations to truly drive inclusive career mapping and ensure that all individuals within an organization have the opportunity to excel within their careers, we need to begin to build sustainable practices for professional growth. At this point we've started to touch on career mapping and its importance in sustaining and developing an organization. Career mapping, however, is just one facet of a broader area of focus—learning and development. Learning and development (which I will refer to from here on out as L&D) encompasses career mapping, but it also extends out to the actual resources and programs that employees can use to help support them as they work to ascend within an organization.

So who should be in charge of L&D? Well I might be a bit biased given my background in DEI, but clearly you're interested in my insight, having made it through nearly half of this book. So let's keep the momentum going! Now back to my question: if you were going to guess the answer is DEI then—ding, ding, ding—you'd be right! Now why is it important that L&D be led by DEI? The answer lies in one-third of the department's responsibilities: inclusion. Typically

L&D has been placed under the people team. However, L&D at its core must focus on inclusivity to ensure that all employees of all backgrounds and levels are given equitable opportunities to advance and develop themselves professionally. L&D platforms and programs need to be focused on inclusion from a process-related standpoint, so it makes sense that it be led by an individual whose concerted focus is on inclusion. I suggest that there be an individual on the DEI team who will focus on L&D principles and practices while expending a strong focus on career mapping. Let's first start out with some L&D principles that should be shared with all employees regardless of professional experience. All individuals should receive focused L&D programming to educate employees about anti-racism efforts, microaggressions, psychological safety, and sexual harassment. These programs should be solution oriented and include accountability measures to help each employee keep themselves and those around them accountable. These are critical trainings that should be shared across all levels, no matter how new or experienced a person is to the workforce.

One main area of career mapping is for effective management: how to do it, how to measure it and how to provide the resources needed by managers to help them sustain and evolve their practices. Without proper training, managers might not be equipped to recognize the different needs and goals of each of their direct reports and can potentially miss the opportunity to help their reports be successful and fulfilled at the organization. I also want to remind you of my earlier point—that management is not the only way to grow within an organization. There are two main pathways an individual can follow: going down a management route or continuing as an individual contributor. I will explore this more in depth shortly but at a broad level, individual contributors are individuals who do not have a team of reports for whom they are responsible, whereas managers will have a team they are responsible for managing. Now for those who are interested in pursuing opportunities in management, the first thing that I will urge managers to do is to practice using inclusive language that will enable each direct report to be seen and understood in real time, allowing the individual the space to fluctuate in their interests, performance, and goals. I recommend that managers set up a practice of homing in on their direct reports' growth trajectories. This means measuring how much an individual has grown over a period of time to pinpoint effort and impactful improvement. I am a huge advocate of empowering people to propel their own growth, and I believe managers can play a huge role in that. Managers should make it very clear to each of their direct reports that they should take the time to examine and identify for themselves what they are doing well at and what they need to improve on. This should be done at the beginning of a person's tenure with the organization and at the end of every review cycle.

Now one important thing to note is that as humans, we are subject to human error. That can include a multitude of things, but for the purpose of this chapter, let's focus on bias. Bias isn't something that is just thrust on other people but rather something that each of us has whether we recognize it or not (but please do try to recognize it). It is near impossible to ask someone to exist bias-free, but what we can ask for is that we constantly challenge ourselves to identify and mitigate bias when it does appear. There are many studies that show trends in self-bias across different backgrounds. For example, there is substantial data that show that white men are far more likely to apply for jobs that they are not fully qualified for. On the flip side, the data also show that if a person of color or woman does not fit every potential requirement for a job description, they are much less likely to still apply for that job than a white man. There are ways in which these biases become internalized and assumed within our self-confidence. This is why the growth trajectory discussion is again a useful conversation. By disregarding inflexible benchmarks and instead looking at the overall growth of an individual, we are able to obtain a more accurate understanding of how a person has progressed. It is important that throughout this process, managers help their direct reports understand and advocate for their development and sidestep any potential self-injected bias.

Organizations should leverage tools that do not incorporate bias and can be used to create balanced teams. If every individual on the team possessed the same strengths and interests, there would be definitive gaps, because *no one* can encompass every skill and strength. Thoughtful and inclusive conversations can enable individual employees to move into roles that they are most happy in and be supported in the process. I recommend that managers use a growth trajectory assessment to be able to track the improvements their direct reports have made. Each direct report will fill out an assessment that will be focused on their current strengths and their areas of improvement. This will be hugely helpful to managers when it comes time for performance reviews because they will have insight into how each individual sees themselves and address any gaps the manager may have noticed. These assessments will also be helpful because performance reviews do not always provide the most equitable and accurate portrayal of each employee. For one, performance reviews tend to take place at the end of the year, which heavily overlaps with the holiday season. Many people take time off during this time or are scrambling to meet their end-of-year deadlines. I was once told by a manager who had a large team that year-end was consistently the most stressful time of year. Work was piling on, deadlines were looming, and on top of that they needed to write up performance reviews for each of their reports. The manager admitted to me that in the midst of all of these responsibilities, if there were certain folks on her team she did not interface with as much, she wasn't able to write a detailed and thoughtful review. By leveraging these assessments, it also frees up managers to have additional resources to reference instead of filling out a year's worth of evaluations in a matter of weeks.

L&D needs to have its own assessment system through the growth trajectory assessments to help illustrate how people benefit from L&D programming and incorporate holistic elements that might go overlooked during a review. These measurements can also enable flexibility for the different situations that can arise professionally or personally. For example, whenever there is an organization change or something occurs in an employee's personal life, it's not unrealistic to see a dip in performance. If organizations rely on strict targets, there is a strong possibility that the employee could be marked as underperforming, when really they were doing their best while navigating additional challenges.

The assessment will be given by each employee's manager and tracked by the DEI L&D specialist and HR. This will ensure that these questionnaires are monitored by multiple people both inside and outside of an employee's vertical to create as many checks and balances as possible.

These questionnaires should be filled out once a year and should be used to demonstrate self-identified growth and assist in sidestepping bias. There is substantial research that shows how certain demographics, especially women and systemically overlooked populations, will be harder on themselves and might rate themselves lower. These questionnaires will also provide an opportunity for employees to amend their initial assessment. For example, someone might have rated themselves very harshly at the beginning of the year, but at the end of the year looking back on their accomplishments would be able to quantify that they might have been stronger in an area than they initially believed and improved even more so. On the flip side, for individuals who have a lot of confidence and may give themselves higher marks from the jump regardless of actual ability (okay, I'll say it: white men), it will be clear to see when they continue to give themselves the same marks at the end of the year. If someone rates themself as excellent in all applicable areas at the beginning of the year and remains excellent without demonstrating any growth, then they did not actually improve at all and that should not be considered successful. No matter at what level an individual is, there is always room for them to grow. If a person is unable to identify the ways in which they've improved, then they should not be promoted. By using these assessments, it becomes less about potential and instead enables each individual to illustrate how much they've truly grown over the year and be able to quantifiably back it up.

How to Incorporate L&D

As we've just discussed, L&D must be placed under DEI so that it can have targeted impact-driven goals that are dynamic and inclusive to all employees, both presently and in the future. Now let's dive into the various types of training that need to take place and are vital to an organization's longevity. L&D trainings and workshops need to be baked into an employee's experience from the beginning stages of onboarding. It's crucial that employees are aware of the resources available to them and the trajectories they can pursue. If an organization has resources prepared and ready to go, they can also be discussed during the hiring process, because this focus is greatly attractive to an individual who is searching for an opportunity in which they can grow and excel. During the onboarding phase, there should be a concerted focus on L&D onboarding and the different opportunities folks can take to grow within the organization. All new employees should participate in mandatory workshops and trainings to learn the impact of L&D and understand how to align it with their growth and performance. I recommend that all content and documentation on L&D be stored in a central location so that all employees can refer back to and access. Managers with direct reports should also include L&D as part of their weekly one-on-ones to further underline the importance of forward thinking and ensure they can assist in advocating for their direct reports' interests.

It will be hugely helpful if organizations take the time to let their DEI L&D specialist sit down and create a comprehensive talent-driven development road map for every vertical and role within the organization. This road map should explicitly list out a full career path within each vertical from the intern or associate level all the way up to the C-Suite level. Every stage will include a list of identified checkboxes of goals each individual must meet in order to achieve a promotion. This creates equitable access to information and opportunity so there are clear-cut expectations on all sides. This road map should be reviewed every promotion cycle so all employees across the board understand the goals and expectations for their new role. It also provides time for each employee to be successful because they have their expectations outlined at the beginning of the year instead of waiting until performance reviews to determine the possibility for promotion.

I've previously worked with a company that did not have an identified career road map and it presented numerous challenges that ended up with the organization losing quite a few excellent employees. The people team, although composed of fantastic individuals, had not been given an opportunity to place priority on identifying these levels and roles. Without these defined growth paths, there was massive confusion that led to inaccurate data about the organizational levels as well as different career trajectories.

It is critical that organizations account for this before they start hiring. It is far more difficult to create career paths retroactively and will be harder to create inclusive career paths. Without establishing this ahead of time, we will see an imbalance in the roles that have clear career paths and those that don't, and a reflective departure of employees. If you are a part of an organization that finds themselves in this predicament, my best advice to you is to spend money on it now. Take the time to do a full diagnostic of the different role levels and career mapping that exists—better yet, hire an external company to come in and build an inclusive career mapping structure. They can help create career tracks for every role and ensure access to training and internal tools that will track participation and completion of these training sessions. It takes people, power, funds, and time, but this is critical to an organization's scalability and employee retention. Basically what I'm saying is call me so that I can help your organization solve bias and build end-to-end direction for all employees.

Building Your Organization's Career Map

So now that we've determined how to create and measure bias-free L&D, how can organizations actually apply these practices? I will walk you through how to break down your organization into professional levels and develop expectations for L&D that can be applied to each employee as they ascend in the organization. Now, this is not one-size-fits-all, so feel free to amend these levels to whatever suits your organization.

For our purposes here, I recommend breaking the organization down into four separate levels. First is the associate level, which will be for early-career employees. Next there is mid-level, which is for employees who are a few years into their profession. The following phase is upper level, which is for employees who are now leaders within the organization and starting to think about departmental strategy. The last and highest level is the executive level, which includes C-Suite individuals.

Now remember back to the beginning of this chapter when I shared the story about the individual who was pushed into an ill-suited role as manager? Well each of these levels will have two potential tracks: one that is more people and managerial focused, and one that is more role focused and enables those who are interested to become experts within their space. It is important to remember that people have different interests; some folks are genuinely interested in investing in other peoples' growth and helping guide their career. Other folks are really passionate about the work they do and want to spend their time becoming experts in their field. Neither choice is wrong; they are simply choices and should have the appropriate opportunities attached to them. Let's go ahead and break down each of these levels to help create a blueprint that you can use to apply to your own organization.

Associate Level

The associate level will comprise entry-level or early-career employees. L&D programming at this level should focus on teaching these individuals how to network, how to practice self-advocacy, and how to find and build relationships with sponsors who can help advocate for their growth. I also recommend offering L&D programs in different areas of interest within the organization. These individuals are earlier in their career, so creating exposure to different pathways or verticals will be most useful to them, because they are newer to the professional space. It can also be useful to help them develop mentorship both inside and outside their direct team so that they can continue to grow their network. I also suggest conducting an overall introduction to all pathways so these associate-level employees can learn about potential different paths they can take.

Mid-Level Individual Contributors and Managers

Once we move up to the mid-level, we will start to break the group down into two sections: individual contributors (ICs) and managers. Mid-level ICs are now focused on specific subject matter and want to remain an IC. They might start to train other individuals in their vertical to share their knowledge and wisdom and will participate in L&D programming that helps them do so effectively. Mid-level ICs could potentially attend conferences or join networks of other ICs across different organizations that are focused on their area of interest. They could start to develop strategies for architecture in their subject matter. They could be responsible for researching and conducting documentation sessions and demos for other folks within their vertical. Essentially, we want mid-level ICs to empower their organizations to carry out the work they do. Their goal is to become an industry expert and share that knowledge with the rest of the organization.

Mid-level managers include any non-senior managers with direct reports. Their L&D programming should be focused on managerial training to learn effective strategies. They should undergo training to understand internal bias across various demographics and how to challenge, support, and advocate for their direct reports using a variety of techniques that suit each of their individual reports. They should also participate in inclusive leadership training and be educated on how to drive and measure DEI KPIs. I strongly recommend that mid-level managers (and up) develop 360-degree feedback to further develop their managerial practices. It's so important for managers to also learn how to receive feedback because this can only make them more effective throughout their career. They should also undergo L&D training that helps them understand different working styles so they can learn how to best support direct reports with different work style preferences and build trust and respect with each of their direct reports. It's also quite important that they conduct individual career mapping with each of their direct reports so that they understand how their direct reports want to grow and ensure that they know the proper steps that must be taken in order to do so. Mid-level managers should also develop inclusive succession planning. Their goal is to be able to quantifiably demonstrate an upward trajectory for both themselves and all of their direct reports. Only if they successfully complete all mid-level managerial training and can illustrate how they've used these trainings to help their direct reports achieve their respective goals are they ready to be promoted to senior manager.

Upper-Level Individual Contributors and Managers

After mid-level ICs are upper-level ICs. This level is made up of folks who, again, do not want to manage but want to continue propelling their vertical and are becoming some of the most knowledgeable people within their vertical. For example, an upper-level IC could be a recruiter who manages a full life cycle but doesn't have any reports; they are in their own lane driving strong impact. At this point, all upper-level ICs should have a strong specialty; they are in essence a subject matter expert with no desire to manage people, but they still want to grow and develop themselves. These should be the individuals who write up the annual behavioral and role-specific questionnaire that will be filled out by all individuals and should participate in L&D training that can help them do so effectively. At this point they are true industry leaders and understand what is needed at associate and mid-level roles, so they can create a rubric for each respective level that will be incorporated into the questionnaire. Upper-level ICs are heavily encouraged to participate and speak at events and/or write up papers and documentation about best practices in their industry. Their primary goal is to ensure processes for mid-level ICs to offer 360-degree feedback to upper-level ICs and derive strategies that can be used to drive business for the organization.

The other side of the level is upper-level management. This will include senior managers, VPs, and SVPs. At this point, these upper-level managers should have success-fully finished all L&D managerial training. They should be focused more on strategy and developing their verti-cal as a whole. Upper-level managers are responsible for tracking current trainings and following up on new tools and metrics that can be leveraged to improve existing pro-cesses. I recommend that all senior-level managers take the time to build relationships with their direct reports' direct reports to stay connected to all individuals across all lev-els within their vertical. Upper-level managers should also support C-Suite strategies through delegating and over-seeing responsibilities. Their primary goal is making sure that everyone in their vertical understands their respec-tive career trajectories and is supported in their endeavors. They should also lead sessions on inclusive practices for the entire organization.

C-Suite Individual Contributors and Managers

The last and highest level within an organization is C-Suite. C-Suite ICs have a pulse on industry knowledge and can introduce impactful trends that can help the organization as a whole. They can also devise their own processes that are adapted by other organizations as well and are true subject matter experts on a domestic or global scale and are driven to make an impact in the work they do. C-Suite managers understand the gaps that exist in various departments and formulate strategies that can positively affect the wider organization and help drive the business successfully. These individuals want to change their world through their work.

Creating these different levels and pathways ensures that people have a path forward at the organization that suits their unique interests and wants. If there is only one provided path forward, then people will be pushed in a direction they may not be interested in and it will set them up for failure and introduce additional challenges for those who work with them. Having a clear set of expectations and opportunities for growth will prevent organizations from inadvertently allowing individuals to cause harm to their peers and the larger organization. Not everyone who is a bad manager is a bad person; they should just be placed where they will be happiest and most effective for the organization.

Sustainable L&D is critical to organizations success at all levels. As I've just outlined, L&D will look different at different levels for ICs and managers, but by offering these resources an organization will be able to retain employees through meaningful growth opportunities, create well-balanced teams, and create positive practices and expectations at an executive level that can be felt across the entire organization.

Chapter 5 Exercise: Designing Inclusive Career Mapping

Career mapping is the thoughtfully constructed pathway of growth with identified goals that an employee can meet in order to develop and ascend within an organization. Inclusive career mapping includes a consideration of an individual's interests and goals to ensure that each employee can work toward a future that they are actively interested in and motivated by. When building out career maps for employees, think about two different tracks: the IC track and a manager track. Each track should have various levels that allow for increasing awareness and complexity within their scope. Each level should clearly address what is expected at that stage and should share the expectations and competencies for moving to the next level so employees know how to progress in their career plan. As employees move up, they should have a culmination of all of the skills at the prior levels.

The Individual Contributor Track

When designing an IC's career map, it's key to first assess the employee's current competencies, knowledge, and skill sets. From there, it's important to incorporate the employee's end goal at the top of the career map so they're excited to continue growing with the organization and feel their efforts are leading them in the direction they wish to grow in. Core competencies and expected outcomes of each role leading up to the final level should be clearly outlined and communicated to the employee. Documentation should outline the full role description, cross-functional reach (what teams and leaders this role will collaborate with), key focus areas, key competencies and mindsets that drive success in the role, and advanced competencies (where they should be per-forming in order to move up). Additionally, for each level, there should be various L&D opportunities that advance in complexity as the levels progress. Managers should have monthly conversations assessing performance and the career mapping plan. Following is a template you can use for the advancement of any IC role. One must simply differentiate the advancement of levels and describe what makes some-one successful in each level.

IC Levels		
Role/Level	Description of role, cross-functional reach, key focus areas, key competencies, advanced competencies	Learning & Development Opportunities
IC Level 1: Entry/ Associate		
IC Level 2: Lead/ Mid		
IC Level 3: Senior/ Principal		
IC Level 4: VP/SVP		
IC Level 5: Executive/ Expert		

The Manager Track

Manager pathways, like those for ICs, should clearly outline the full role description, cross-functional reach, key focus areas, key competencies, advanced competencies, L&D opportunities, *and* management and inclusive leadership training courses. Following is a manager track template to complete for each employee. Remember that every employee's career pathway may look different depending on the individual's personal goals. The most important thing is that there are clear expectations of success in the role and opportunities to learn and grow beyond any current level.

Management Track Levels			
Role/Level	Description of Role, Cross-Functional Reach, Key Focus Areas, Key Competencies, Advanced Competencies	L&D Opportunities	Management & Inclusive Leadership Training
Manager Level 1: **Entry/ Associate**	Manager in training		
Manager Level 2: **Manager Title**	Has at least one direct report		

(*Continued*)

Management Track Levels			
Role/Level	Description of Role, Cross-Functional Reach, Key Focus Areas, Key Competencies, Advanced Competencies	L&D Opportunities	Management & Inclusive Leadership Training
Manager Level 3: **Senior/ Director**	Has a team		
Manager Level 4: **VP/SVP**	Has teams leading teams, focused on strategy		
Manager Level 5: **Executive/ C Suite**	Focused primarily on strategy		

In every role within the organization, remember every employee deserves an individual development plan, consistent and thoughtful feedback through one-on-one meetings, opportunities to increase knowledge and complexity, and a clear pathway to an advanced role.

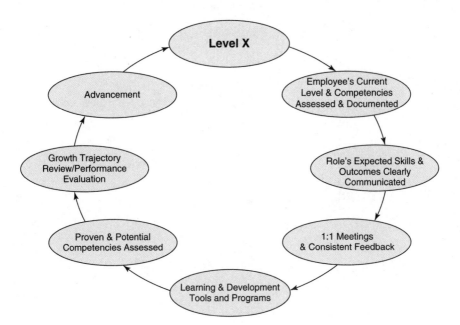

6

Are Your Policies Powerful or Powerless?

YEARS AGO WHEN I was still a bit newer to the workforce, I got the opportunity I had always dreamed of: to be able to travel for work. Now don't get me wrong, I wasn't excited about the prospect of working, but I was definitely excited about the ability to travel with colleagues and let our hair down to enjoy the after-hours. I always imagined that as my career grew it would take me to different places and enable me to learn and connect with people outside of my immediate day-to-day. When I was finally given the opportunity for the first time, I jumped at the chance. I was ready to enjoy my business class seat on an airline (see you later, economy!), don my plush hotel robe, and enjoy a fresh king-size bed all for myself. I was about to pack and jet when my manager uttered a sentence to me that instantly deflated my excitement. "Alright, Netta, go ahead and book your flight and hotel and you'll get the reimbursement in your next check." My heart dropped. Now I don't know about you, but I didn't always have the ability to book a flight and hotel stay at any given moment. At that time in my life, I was already dealing with the stress of supporting my family and paying off student loans (which I'm still paying off by the way). So to put it in other terms, had I tried to charge the expenses to my credit card, it would've bounced like a house (bouncy house). I had no other choice but to work up the courage to go to my manager and let them know that I didn't have the means to pay for the trip and flight out of my own pocket. It was humiliating and nerve-wracking, and honestly if I didn't have the connection I did with my manager, I'm not sure how I would've navigated that conversation. Although my manager was very kind and understanding, there still wasn't an easy, clear-cut solution. My company had to find a specialized credit card that would enable me to use company funds to cover the cost of the trip. It required looping in the accounting department, getting a sign-off from the CEO, and then notifying the parent company and their respective departments. One small issue suddenly became a much bigger one with so many people who had to get involved in the process. All of this only added to my stress and embarrassment of the situation, all of which could have been avoided had there been better processes in place to support employees and insulate them from having to pay up-front company costs.

I recognize that my story, as humbling as it was, is still one of privilege. Being able to travel for work when I didn't have two toddlers, as demanding or strenuous as it can be even as a non-caregiver, is still a huge privilege. But this isn't the only situation in which people find themselves struggling even in the midst of being employed. One of my close friends went through a period of homelessness while they were working a steady, full-time job. They were one of millions of Americans who are dealing with the formidable weight of student loans that continue to rack up inhumane levels of interest. My friend was faced with the decision of doing everything they could to pay down their debt to keep it from accruing or being able to pay rent. They ended up forfeiting their apartment and had to live out of their car so that their income could go toward their student loan debt. This is the unfortunate reality that so many Americans face—people have to decide if they are going to be able to eat or have somewhere to lay their heads at night, or pay off their debt, bills, childcare, and so on. The list unfortunately goes on and on.

Why am I sharing these stories? Well it's because so many Americans who are hard-working and dedicated employees are still struggling to make ends meet and take care of all of their needs, even while being incredibly responsible and thoughtful. But with some concerted support from organizations, so many of these issues can be addressed and lead to increased happiness and productivity both inside and outside of the workplace. That brings me to the topic of this chapter: helping organizations pursue and develop inclusive policies.

How to Support Your Employees

One of the most common questions I get asked by organization leaders is about the future of policies and how to leverage policies to build increased employee satisfaction and retention. I have sectioned these policies into four main areas that organizations can use to build comprehensive policies and benefits to provide the most holistic and productive support for their employees. Without an intentional focus on these areas, organizations at best run the risk of losing employees who do not feel like they are receiving adequate support, and at worst open themselves to the potential of lawsuits, because inequitable care could legitimately be argued to be discriminative. The amount of money an organization could spend fighting lawsuits would be much better spent on developing policies that help retain and appeal to talent to build a diverse organization. Developing inclusive policies would also enable organizations to highlight and demonstrate their investment in equity as well as illustrate their commitment to providing psychological safety for their employees. These are critical factors in driving retention and supporting recruiting processes. Although these efforts won't be financially light, they are an important investment organizations will be happy they made down the line.

The four areas that I recommend organizations use as a starting point for developing inclusive policies are flexibility, health care, caregiving, and growth and development. This list is of course nonexhaustive and can absolutely be tailored to fit your particular organization, which I will share more about shortly. For now, let's dive into each of these areas further.

Flexible Policies

It's no secret that one of the biggest changes organizations have had to tackle as of lately has been the coronavirus. The pandemic turned the entire world upside down and left organizations scrambling with how to continue operations with the majority of the workforce transitioning to remote work.

This led to a dissolution of areas of life—work life and personal life became intertwined as people lost the ability to leave their houses while continuing with their day-to-day responsibilities as an employee and the other multitude of hats they wore. Although we've started to see the promise of a safer future, it's very likely that things will never fully go back to the way they were, and it's important that organizations evolve alongside these global changes.

All organizations should provide each of their employees the option to select their working situation. Employees should be able to choose between working fully remote, a hybrid situation in which they are sometimes remote and sometimes in the office, or being able to come into the office and work as they please. Every person has their own particular situation that would most enable them to be productive and support their personal needs, and they should be allowed to set up their work situation accordingly. For some individuals, coming into the office can be taxing and challenging. I once knew a family who had two young children in preschool. Although both parents were initially working full-time, they decided that one parent would quit their job to stay home and take care of their children since their entire paycheck was going toward covering the costs of preschool. It ended up making more financial sense for them to live off of one income and be able to be home and spend more time with their child. Had they been given the option to work remotely, they could have had the potential to create a situation in which they could both help out with their children while keeping both income streams. Other people really enjoy coming into the workplace and having the opportunity to create a bit of separation between their personal time at home and their time at work. Maybe they really enjoy the casual chats that come from being around people in the office, or they want to take advantage of some of the office perks, whether it be lunches, events, or even just space for a comfortable desk. What's most important is that each employee should be empowered to decide what path works best for them and have the support and flexibility of their organization in doing so.

Another policy I strongly recommend organizations adopting is that of a flexible work day. As many organizations are now offering options for fully remote or hybrid roles, people are starting to see the benefits of having more control over their time. Allowing employees to have increased flexibility in the work day, from scheduling preferences to teams working across different time zones, this flexibility enables people to be in control of their personal and familial responsibilities while maintaining high levels of productivity. In a similar vein, any companies that offer remote or hybrid opportunities should offer a home office stipend to ensure their employees have access to anything they would need to do their job successfully.

Going back to my personal experience from the beginning of the chapter, organizations need to come up with more streamlined processes for reimbursement. Employees should never be expected to pay for organizational costs up-front, regardless of their title or level within the organization. It should never be assumed that individuals at higher income brackets are financially stress-free and able to take on up-front payments. Every individual has their own financial responsibilities and should be equitably provided reimbursements. There are many companies that actually focus on this area and work to create a hassle-free process for employees who have to make purchases on their organization's behalf. For example, I've worked with a company called Teampay that provides virtual, preloaded cards for employees that pull directly from company funds. It ensures that employees will never have to pay out of pocket, and it leverages an approval process between a direct report and their manager. While using Teampay, I've been able to pay securely and instantly while being spared the shame and trouble I encountered all those years ago. Last, I strongly recommend that organizations offer unlimited PTO with a required minimum of days employees need to take off. There is substantial data that suggest that when organizations adopt an unlimited PTO policy, employees can oftentimes end up taking less PTO than they would if they were given a set amount of days. Folks can become afraid to take PTO depending on the company culture and how it can trickle down the ranks. Especially as there has been a massive shift to remote work, boundaries get blurred when people work from home, and it can be easy to lose a sense of balance or separation between professional life and personal life. Managers and HR should work together to monitor the PTO taken by each individual, and if certain folks aren't taking enough PTO, the individual should be told to take some time off to make sure they hit the minimum PTO requirement. Their respective team should work together to make sure all deadlines are met in their absence and nothing falls behind, but it is so important that each individual feels important and supported by their organization and is given dedicated time to rest and refresh. By ensuring employees have the freedom and flexibility to take care of their personal lives and are mandated to use it, organizations are able to facilitate better self-care for their employees, which leads to higher happiness and appreciation.

Basic Human Rights Policy

Perhaps one of the most integral policies that an organization must offer is for inclusive health care policies. People oftentimes literally work to live, and without good health care they can become unable to do either. Health care is not just an additional benefit; it is and should always be seen as a basic human right. Health care is one of the more common benefits currently offered by employers, but the pandemic has highlighted a couple of critical gaps that need to be supported moving forward. Again, as organizations move toward remote or hybrid working policies, health care services must also reflect that level of flexibility. Organizations should include options for telehealth and virtual health care services that enable their employees to receive medical care from the comfort of their home when applicable and so that people can safely receive medical support in a timely manner.

My next point, and I can't stress this enough, is that mental health coverage is just as important as physical health and requires the full coverage that is given to physical, dental, and vision. Especially in the wake of the pandemic, an increased coverage of longstanding police brutality, violence and killings of communities of color, while watching all of this unfold from the confinement of our homes, a serious toll has been taken on our collective mental health. Employers need to offer mental health care coverage, with options for virtual support. As a DEI executive leader, I strongly advise that organizations take the following steps during times of trauma and tragedy to lend additional support to their employees. When possible, organizations should simply shut down. Traumatizing events take time to process, and it can be incredibly challenging to try and maintain a typical workday as if something horrible hasn't just happened. It gives employees the time to process and grieve and not exude a level of inauthenticity as they fight to pretend like they aren't reeling from recent events while going through the typical motion of meetings, agendas, and professional chitchat. If that simply isn't possible for the organization to do as a whole, then organizations should definitely encourage managers to check in with each of their direct reports and shift deadlines to give people more time to complete their work, understanding that productivity will likely not be as high during this time. Last, organizations should bring in DEI professionals or psychologists who can lead healing sessions and specialize in trauma and grief work. We are far past the time of pretending that we as humans exist in professional silos. We are layered and holistic people who are very much affected by the ongoings around us, and when organizations can celebrate and support their employees as such, deeper trust and mutual respect can grow.

Caregiving

More likely than not, organizations will have employees who are taking care of other individuals in addition to themselves. They could have spouses, children, or older relatives that require their care and attention. Organizations should ensure that they include policies that support those employees in a caregiving position so that they are able to maintain their personal responsibilities alongside their professional ones. First and foremost, organizations should offer both maternity and paternity leave for parents of equal duration to ensure equitable time off for new parents. These policies should extend to LGBTQIA+ families as well and should be flexible enough to adapt to all family types and situations. IVF and family planning should also be covered as part of the benefits package. In the event that the insurance that the organization selects doesn't cover IVF and family planning, then the organization should offer a stipend of up to 50% of all health care–related costs to provide equitable support to all families.

As a mom of two myself, I know firsthand how costly childcare can get and how it can create a more economically fragile home. The irony isn't lost on me that some parents have to work to pay for childcare, as opposed to having to put their children in childcare to be able to work. I recommend that organizations offer at least a $200/month stipend towards childcare (with the understanding that childcare can easily add up to a few grand a month).

Caregiving policies should also cover family leave and bereavement leave, giving employees the opportunity and support to care for their family members. These policies should be flexible enough that all people and families are offered the same level of protection and benefits regardless of state-wide legislation. For example, a same-sex couple in a state that may not recognize their union should still receive the same full benefits and support as another heteronormative couple through the organization. Last, there is an imperative for confidentiality for any employee who may take advantage of any of these benefits. These resources should be offered hassle-free without the need for excessive appeals or requests; employees should have access to these benefits with their confidentiality respected and a stringent need-to-know basis for any individuals within the organization who would have to help facilitate the process.

Growth and Development

Another important focus of inclusive policies is for growth and development. Organizations should directly invest in their employees' growth and provide access to resources that will enable each of their employees to expand on their skill sets and knowledge. I recommend organizations provide each employee with an annual learning stipend that can be used at each individual's discretion to focus on a role-related interest. Individuals could use this stipend toward learning courses and materials, attending conferences, or participating in networking events. By providing financial support toward their employees' development, organizations are able to support and facilitate expanding on their employees' curiosity and knowledge. I also recommend that organizations provide a stipend toward college loans. The average college debt for an American in 2022 is about $33,000, with a good portion of the population with debt in the six-figure range. Student loans can be an extremely costly personal expense, and organizations can help offset some of that stress through offering this stipend.

The What's Next Assessment

Above all, good policies are about organizations being proactive in thinking about the safety and needs of their employees as they continue to drive increased representation.

Although these areas I outlined are good foundations to start with, I understand that not all organizations are in a financial place to offer each of these policies. What all organizations can do, however, is figure out their particular starting point. My strongest recommendation when working with anyone, whether it be your own employees, your clients, or partners, is to figure out where they are at and meet them there. Ask your employees directly which benefits would be most valuable to them and aggregate this data to understand the benefits that would have the most impact across the organization. I recommend sharing an annual assessment of the possibilities of benefits and ask each employee to select their top three. This will provide insight into the most meaningful resources that will help employees feel valued and supported inside and outside of their job functions. By conducting this assessment on an annual basis, it will communicate to leaders if there is a shift in priorities and will enable the organization to respond accordingly.

One last thing I want to note is that although these benefits largely pertain to full-time employees, when an organization is thinking about offering these policies, don't forget about the consultants, part-time workers, contractors, or those who help maintain the office space. If an organization is unable to provide full benefits for these groups the way they would full-time salaried roles, explore more creative options such as stipends that could provide a similar benefit. Especially consider that each of these individuals is a potential future employee who, if brought on, would greatly mitigate onboarding and training costs. Building an inclusive organization includes all different types of employees, and leadership should think about ways to provide subsidized resources for different employee groups to ensure that these policies are equitable in both practice and execution.

Chapter 6 Exercise: The What's Next Assessment

Now it's your turn to take what you've learned in this chapter and turn it into actionable steps. Think about the policies you want to see incorporated into your organization's practices.

Reflection

Review the following policies. Place a checkmark beside every policy your organization has implemented and circle those you wish to see implemented.

- ☐ Remote work policy
- ☐ Flexible work day policy
- ☐ Reimbursement policy
- ☐ Unlimited PTO policy
- ☐ Health care coverage for employees and families
- ☐ Mental health coverage
- ☐ Telehealth and virtual health care service
- ☐ Parental leave for new parents
- ☐ IVF and family planning coverage or stipends
- ☐ Family leave and bereavement leave policy
- ☐ Annual learning stipends
- ☐ Student loan relief

Answer the following questions to support your case for introducing new people policies.

What are the top three policies (either implemented or not at your organization) that are most meaningful to you and why?	
What inclusive policies has your organization currently implemented that you are most proud of?	
Where is your organization lacking and how can it do better?	

Assessment

In order to implement policies that are truly beneficial to your organization, you first need to understand what is most important to your employees by conducting an assessment. What is the demographic makeup of your employees? What do folks value the most when it comes to benefits and policies that serve to protect them? If your organization is looking to embed more inclusivity into its current practices and policies, the best way to prioritize next steps is to ask for feedback from your employees. I recommend conducting an inclusive policy assessment and surveying employees on identity, priorities, and potential organizational gaps.

In this assessment it's key to ask employees about how they choose to identify, intersectionalities, and policies that are most important to them. You should ask questions assessing one's personal needs and poll the desire for various inclusive policies mentioned in this chapter. I also recommend creating this assessment with open-ended questions so folks can add as much detail as they wish, as well as include any other identities they wish to include with their responses.

Assessment Criteria
- Self-identification (gender, race, ethnicity, age)
- Employee's unique intersectionalities (caregiver status, veteran status, LGBTQIA+ status, visible or invisible disabilities)
- Employee status (full-time employee, part-time employee, contractor, consultant)
- Desired working hours
- Workspace preference (office setting, remote setting, or a hybrid setting)

- Policy needs as it pertains to
  - Health care
  - Telehealth and virtual health care
  - PTO
  - Retirement
  - Bereavement leave, family leave
  - Flexibility
  - Mental health resources
  - Wellness
  - Student loans
  - Learning stipends
  - Caregiving
  - Family planning
  - Childcare
  - Reimbursement
  - Travel benefits/expenses

Post-Assessment

After you have valuable data points regarding your organization's employees, their demographics, and your potential blind spots, answer the following questions:

What steps are you going to take to advocate for the policies most important to you and your employees within your organization?	
Write down senior leaders, ERGs leaders, people team members, third-party vendors, or board members who you will leverage to support these efforts.	

7

Diversity Recruiting

LET'S KICK THIS off with a little exercise of pretend, shall we? Let's imagine that in this situation, you are not you, and I am not me. We are simply two attendees at an annual gala hosted by a nonprofit we both happen to work with. I was invited to speak at the gala, and you were excited to have a chance to chat as we both work in the same field and you were already familiar with my work. The night of the gala you approached me after my speech to congratulate me and introduce yourself, but I brushed you off, literally walking past your extended arm before you could even get out "hello." I walked right by you smiling while I extended my hand to shake the hand of the person behind you, as if you weren't even there. To put it mildly, I left a bit to be desired in interpersonal skills. To put it accurately, well, I was a bit of an arrogant jerk. The day after the gala, I had lunch with the founder of the nonprofit when I mentioned one of my current ongoing projects that had been giving me a bit of grief. She was surprised—apparently there was a guest at last night's gala who actually specialized in the exact area I was struggling in, and she thought we would have connected given our shared work and interests. Surprise, surprise—that guest was you! The stranger I rudely ignored all night. She gave me your contact info so I could reach out later. Now, what would you do if you received that call from me? Well, if you're anything like me, you might laugh into the phone and hang up immediately. Well, no, I'm just kidding, I probably wouldn't do that. But I may want to.

The point of this exercise is really just to say that true inclusion is identifying the power you hold at all times and sharing with others. Inclusion is practiced before incentive and with thoughtfulness and consistency. It is not an afterthought, and the same way you probably felt a bit slighted and indignant during our exercise when you were so rudely ignored, my calling you the following day with flowery words of patronizing compliments probably would not do much to improve your opinion of me. So it's safe to assume that neither do retroactive performative gestures. Real feelings can be found in our daily actions, in how we live out our relationships and how we choose to connect with one another.

Proactively Building a Pipeline

So how can organizations start to build intentional relationships that support their efforts to be equitable and inclusive? I will provide you with five results-driven, creative ways to increase diversity, but this isn't an exhaustive list. The first step is making sure the organization is connected to individuals that can help drive impact to achieve those goals. These connections can be built through the process of diversity recruiting. I define *diversity recruiting* as an organization assessing the lack of a specific identity, be it race or ethnicity or gender, within the organization, with an intersectional lens. Once these gaps have been identified, the organization then makes intentional efforts to develop recruiting strategies aimed at mitigating those gaps. Just to be frank, these gaps most often affect Black+, Hispanic/Latinx+, Asian+, and Indigenous+ populations, with intersectionalities that can include woman-identifying or nonbinary, LGBTQIA+, veterans, caregivers, and/or differently abled populations as well. These gaps can also exist on organizational levels, with the organizations seeing more homogenous patterns as one ascends the organization's ladder. Organizations are more productive, psychologically safe, and profitable (I know some ears perked up there!) when there is equitable representation across and within the organization, and diversity recruiting is an excellent place to start.

It can be exceptionally powerful for organizations to proactively demonstrate their commitment to building equitably and inclusively. A great and direct way organizations can do this is by having their systemically overlooked employees share which organizational benefits were most integral in helping them decide to join the company. Benefits are a great resource in exciting potential candidates, and there are four areas of benefits I encourage organizations to pursue. The first thing an organization can do is provide concrete examples of the ways in which it has actively worked against racial disparity within the organization. This cannot be emphasized enough—recruiters should be able to share examples of how the organization addressed previous disparities and how the current policies and practices prevent future discrepancies from occurring. For example, the organization can share how it uses market rates to determine salaries. If the organization truly feels that their employees are valuable, then they will want to compensate them accordingly. Perhaps the organization even has quarterly pay audits conducted by external organizations to ensure that pay is equitable across identities and levels. Through specific and transparent examples, recruiters will be able to demonstrate the organization's commitment and proactivity in fighting racial injustice. Another benefit organizations can offer is fully remote work. Fully remote opportunities can be highly attractive, especially for systematically overlooked populations. It alleviates the physical microaggressions or stressors that certain populations encounter in the workplace and instead enables them to work from the comfort and safety of their own home. Employees don't need to put in the extra effort or mental preparation of the stress of dealing with interpersonal nuances if they do not feel comfortable doing so. For those who feel a level of safety in their own space, they are supported in working productively from that space in a way that works for them. Organizations should also look into creating care stipends—a stipend outside of paychecks that can help support some of the bills or expenses employees might have. I've seen organizations provide stipends to help cover Wi-Fi, phone bills, rent, or student loans. Last, organizations can create a sponsorship program (which is different from a mentorship program). Sponsorship programs assign an executive leader to a few folks from systemically overlooked populations who are interested in joining this program. From there, the executive leaders follow these individuals throughout their career and advocate for them to help them receive recognition and drive their careers in the ways they want.

Now as our story at the beginning of the chapter mentioned, in order for relationship building to be truly meaningful and sustainable, it takes proactive effort and time. No matter what role one holds within an organization, or how new or familiar one may be to their company, if individuals are truly focused on DEI, then there must be an emphasis on building a diverse and inclusive pipeline. So how can organizations be proactive in building such a pipeline? Well, it can start as simply as whom they work with. Does the organization have at least one diversity supplier? A diversity supplier is a business you work or partner with that is either owned by someone from a systemically overlooked background or is at least 51% operated by individuals from systemically overlooked backgrounds. Organizations should take a look at their current recruiting partners and recruiting platform vendors and identify the businesses with which they could partner as their diversity supplier. As a side note, if your organization has the opportunity to work with a startup, a statistic you might find interesting is that women-led start-ups receive only 2.2% of all venture capital funding, with women of color receiving below 0.2% of all venture capital funding. And once these partnerships have been built, don't let the momentum stop there. Introduce the organization's diversity recruiting suppliers to the organization's funders and investors. Invite them to board meetings and galas and fundraisers. Position the organization to act as the dot connector by opening its network to amplify and drive business toward its diversity suppliers. And needless to say, if the organization doesn't have a diversity supplier, well, they darn well better go find one! There's already a lack of funding and cash flow into these suppliers, so one way to even the playing field is by distributing funding and partnerships to those who have been most vulnerable. That diversity partner or vendor will do everything in their power to help you increase representation because you've helped and developed a strong relationship.

I'm usually a pretty strong advocate of not reinventing the wheel, especially when it already works so well. The same idea rings true here; the second tactic organizations can use in proactively building a pipeline is supporting efforts that are already underway in tackling systemic gaps. Support organizations or attend conferences and summits that are already working with (and often led by) systemically overlooked populations. An organization called Sista Circle: Black Women in Tech is a community for Black+ women in tech to connect and share employment opportunities. Organizations like Sista Circle can leverage communities and help specifically to increase Black representation. Or, events like Afrotech will create access to an exceptional network of curious and capable folks from different systemically overlooked backgrounds. However, simply attending such events with nothing but a list of names and emails will yield no impactful results. The point is to build a pipeline, and that—like Rome—wasn't built in a day. Communication and relationships take time and effort, but when the time comes, these relationships and lines of communication will enable the organization to tap in folks who will be able to contribute and greatly enhance the organization's work.

Organizations should also join Dipper, a digital platform with a member base composed of Black+, Latinx+, Asian, and Indigenous professionals. Organizations can use their Dipper membership to create their organizational DEI profile to highlight and share their benefits and DEI efforts as well as share open and upcoming roles. I've also created a new LinkedIn live show called "Hiring Manager Hotline" that is focused on helping hiring managers fill their open roles. The "Hiring Manager Hotline" has two hiring managers from different companies pitch their open roles to a LinkedIn live online audience of over 200k followers. The hiring managers will be asked six rapid-fire questions that job seekers are most interested in having answered. Job seekers tune in and have the opportunity to learn about the role from the role's manager to learn more about the opportunity, their potential manager, and their leadership practices. This has been a very successful show and has helped numerous hiring managers fill their open roles with attendees from the show.

The third thing organizations can do is create an external Slack community for applicants. Participants can view new open roles, connect with hiring managers, and speak with different employee resource groups (ERGs) to learn more about the work and have a chance to learn more about the organization's culture. This external Slack community could be a great resource for the individuals the organization want to apply. By giving these folks access to the organization's community, it greatly increases the chances of them applying. This community would be open to potential applicants or folks who have already applied and weren't selected—specifically those who made a positive impression but perhaps weren't great for the role they applied for at that time. Just because they weren't selected for that initial role doesn't mean they can't be an asset to the organization at a later date or in a different role. By focusing on providing exposure and expanding connections, organizations are able to invest in attracting resourceful and intrigued candidates who would strongly appreciate the organization's efforts in intentional recruiting.

It Takes All of Us

So we've discussed a few ways in which this inclusive pipeline can be enacted on an organizational level. But these responsibilities don't just exist on an organizational level; they are also needed on a personal level, in our day-to-day life. All employees are part of creating and maintaining this business pipeline, especially managers with direct reports. Managers with direct reports are responsible for facilitating the growth and development of each of their team members, as well as making decisions in the hiring process for new employees. Therefore, it makes sense that these individuals have the ability to be huge drivers in creating a pipeline. I recommend that each of these managers makes a concerted effort to attend conferences and events that are targeted toward systemically overlooked populations, *especially* if the manager themself does not identify as part of the population. Why, you might ask? Well, for one, it will be a strong learning experience for the manager to connect with people they might not typically be in the same spaces as, and two, it will be humbling to finally understand what it's like to be "othered" just on entering a room. It may provide some insight and empathy into the experiences of systemically overlooked populations who consistently find themselves being the only when they enter spaces and have to navigate code-switching, microaggressions, and all the other challenges that come along when one is the minority within a space.

Managers should track the conferences they attend, and this information should be shared across the organization. Every person in the organization should have access to data about the roles the organization is hiring for, the conferences folks have attended, and the individuals from those conferences who would be great potential candidates for the organization. ICs can support their managers by staying aligned with and aware of their managers' efforts and adding a level of value to the pipeline-building process, even if the team doesn't currently have an active headcount. After all, isn't that what being proactive is? Preparing for something before you need it?

One last thing I'd be remiss if I didn't mention is that the organization must ensure that their recruiting team itself is diverse and representative; otherwise, a lot of these other efforts may fall a bit flat. It isn't enough that recruiters are being trained in inclusion and bias-free practices, it is imperative that the recruiting team is composed of individuals who are able to identify *and* disrupt the systems at play that are designed to benefit the privileged majority, and they can do so by intimately understanding these challenges for themselves. Recruiters from systemically overlooked backgrounds are more likely to understand the insidious barriers that exist within commonly leveraged recruitment practices that end up creating non-inclusive practices, such as arbitrary education requirements, experience-based vernacular in job descriptions, or only posting jobs to certain websites that allow candidates to pay for premium experiences. Furthermore, these recruiters may be able to speak more directly and comfortably with candidates who are concerned about how the organization handles inclusion from the perspective of someone who can actually understand their concerns. These experiences commonly shared by overlooked populations obviously cannot be taught, but that doesn't mean these experiences don't exist and play a major role in perpetuating inequity throughout the recruitment process.

The Life Cycle of Recruiting

The recruiting life cycle is a holistic process that actually begins long before the job descriptions get shared with the general public. There are many internal decisions that have to take place prior to actively seeking out potential candidates.

Phase 1: Headcount

The first step within the recruiting life cycle is determining how many individuals the organization is looking to hire, and which teams these individuals will be hired for. Typically, the finance department will assess what the headcount for the upcoming year looks like based on the organization's financial outlook. Based on these numbers, HR and DEI should partner with applicable department heads to assess the managers who will add to their team. This process will provide two separate outcomes. The first will be determining which manager is able to add to their team and the second is an opportunity for HR and DEI to carry out an additional check to make sure all managers are being thoughtful and inclusive leaders and will continue leading their teams as such. I strongly recommend that the DEI and HR teams work together to pull data from annual reviews and exit interviews to see if any managers have red flags concerning their leadership style and impact. HR and

DEI can use this information to assess if all managers have been conducting themselves in an inclusive and supportive manner with each of their direct reports. For example, HR needs to identify why people may have left each manager's team by reviewing exit interviews. If folks left due to mistreatment by that manager, then that manager should not be given additional headcount. In fact, the manager should be placed on a behavioral improvement plan, and if they don't improve, then they should be removed from the company. These individuals are not adding value and in fact are hurting the organization from a financial perspective. This annual process should be baked into policies from the onboarding stage so managers understand there will be 360-degree feedback and that the organization has a zero-tolerance policy for non-inclusive leaders, which includes leaders who lack the ability to respect, support, empathize, or value the contributions of those who are different from them. Perhaps these non-inclusive leaders were biased, controlling, perpetuated selective favoritism, or exhibited a lack of self-accountability. The bottom line is that the cost of non-inclusive leadership is pricey. According to *Huffington Post*, between stress-related health expenses, discrimination lawsuits, productivity losses, and the costs associated with high employee turnover rates, non-inclusive leaders are hemorrhaging an estimated $360 billion each year from US organizations. Have you ever witnessed a colleague (or even yourself) seem to be mentally checked out, self-isolating, or unresponsive to requests? When we think of examples of non-inclusive leadership, a lot of us tend to think about blatant examples like a colleague getting berated in front of everyone in the office or a manager belittling their subordinate's opinions and ideas in an all-staff meeting. But there are more subtle ways in which these transgressions can occur. One example is a manager demanding a project get completed the same day it is given out without regard for the person's workload, or leaving a particular person or group out of decision-making with the excuse that things will move faster if limited to the selected individuals. Another example is a manager assigning a task without clearly defining what the person is to achieve or what the expectations are, and when asked for clarity, the answer is one of those snarky "I hired you to figure it out" responses. *Forbes* shared that on average it takes people 22 months (almost 2 years) to restore stress levels to a healthy range after a non-inclusive experience? Organizations where this type of management occurs have a copious number of unhealthy employees who are oftentimes working while experiencing work-related PTSD. In fact, research proves that women are more likely than men to experience this phenomenon, with higher levels experienced by racialized employees. This is why the process to determine headcount can be strategized as an invaluable opportunity to confirm that all leaders are managing inclusively.

Once all managers have been reviewed and the teams who will be given headcount are identified, the hiring manager should decide ahead of time how the headcount will be broken up. For example, a hiring manager could decide to dedicate 50% of their headcount to individuals who have proven ability in the open role. This could look like applicants who have had significant prior experience handling the role's responsibilities and would require less role-based training on joining the team. In this case, the hiring manager would devote the other 50% of the headcount to individuals with strong potential: those who may not have all the bells and whistles on their résumés or years of experience within the industry, but instead are engaging, curious, motivated, and have transferable skills from other areas of their lives. Now it's important to note that these breakdowns should span across levels and demographics. This should definitely not look like categorizing systemically overlooked populations as feeders for roles designated for potential. There should be some senior roles that are given to candidates with strong potential, and there should be junior roles that will be filled by those who have had experience in the industry—it should be evenly spread. By allocating this breakdown ahead of time, the hiring manager will be able to strengthen the team based on organizational need while also bringing in fresh perspectives who will have the opportunities to grow and enhance the team's impact overall in a fair and equitable way.

Phase 2: Creating a Job Description

Now that headcount has been established and each team has an overall hiring strategy, the next step is sharing the roles and their respective responsibilities so that applicants can start applying. This is typically done through a job description, but there are a number of ways in which an organization can ensure that the job descriptions they share with the general public are inclusive and able to attract the candidates they are looking for. First and foremost, there must be standardized language across all job descriptions that clearly outlines the company's values, responsibilities, and commitment to DEI. By uniformly including this in each job description, the organization is able to demonstrate the strong cultural value it places on equity and inclusion. For example (and feel free to recycle this!), an organization can put the following language into each job description:

> At [COMPANY NAME], one of our values is *Inclusion*. DEI efforts are tied directly to performance and all employees are responsible for one goal that is worked on for the year. These goals help us drive representation, greater retention, and inclusion for all.

The "Responsibility" section for each role will include a bullet point of the DEI responsibilities expected of each employee. This will demonstrate that DEI efforts are not separate from any particular role or function but instead are embedded into the day-to-day of each employee. Your organization may not have a DEI tracking system, but if you're interested in that, contact me because I've created a platform that does this for companies. If your organization has budget constraints, then you can track DEI in an Excel spreadsheet that all employees have access to. This bullet point could read as follows:

> Responsibility: On an annual basis, commit to your team's DEI KPI pillar, deliver on one or more KPI goals, and track them in the DEI KPI application driving DEI impact.

It's also incredibly important that all job descriptions feature inclusive language. For many applicants, the job description may be their first interaction with an organization, and not having inclusive language could turn away candidates before they even throw their hat in the ring. There are a number of organizations that focus on providing augmented writing tools that assess language inclusivity and offer suggestions for language that is not inclusive. I recommend organizations do their research and use these tools for every job description (or marketing piece) they put out. These tools should be used consistently because language is dynamic and we are constantly learning and unlearning ways in which to speak and communicate inclusively.

I also recommend that organizations take the time to assess which job requirements are truly requirements and which are just arbitrary statements that are copied and pasted without serious regard or necessity. Does this role truly and unequivocally require a degree? Or could someone who perhaps is currently in school part-time, or someone who taught themselves technical skills beyond what they could have learned in a few introductory courses, do as good a job or even better a job than someone with their degree? If any of these examples (or others) could be the case, then take off the educational requirement. You risk losing creative and hardworking individuals otherwise. An arbitrary and silly requirement I've heard comes from engineers who have shared that they had seen job descriptions that asked for 10+ years of experience in a language or framework that had only been around for 3 to 4 years. Such missteps are laughable and honestly a bit lazy, and again can cause you to lose talented, impactful applicants. It's so important that each requirement on every job description is carefully and thoughtfully reviewed to most accurately describe the qualifications that will allow a person to be successful at the role described. I personally like the idea of separating job *requirements* from *nice-to-haves*. Certain things may be nonnegotiable, but many things, I'm sure, are not.

In today's competitive market, organizations should take the time to share with applicants what they have to gain if they join the organization. I recommend that job descriptions include additional sections that describe what applicants will learn in this role and how they will be able to grow, both personally and professionally. Job descriptions should also include the organization's most inclusive benefits to illustrate how the organization is especially thoughtful and intentional in considering their employees' needs. I've already shared a number of these benefits, but I will reiterate how critical it is to also share how employees have been able to use these benefits and the impact these benefits have had. For example, the organization can share information about their childcare policy and how a percentage of employees have used this assistance to cover daycare for their kids enabling them not to pay for daycare assistance, simply to work. Or, the organization can share how employees have used the gender reassignment health care policy to cover their health care costs during their transition. This personal element will demonstrate that the organization truly cares about their employees and wants to make sure they are supported both inside and outside of work. Wouldn't you want to work for an organization that went to this length to demonstrate that it cares and that employees feel comfortable using the benefits?

Oh, and please, *please* include the salary range. Not only is it now illegal to withhold that information in some US states but it also perpetuates the massive inequity that exists during the negotiation process. Especially when there are substantial trends of folks from systemically overlooked backgrounds asking for less (because they might not be aware of what other more privileged applicants feel comfortable asking for), it is so important that this information is made public so that all applicants understand a respectable and realistic range to ask for. Gone are the days of stale job descriptions—it takes more now to attract candidates. It will only benefit the organization to make each candidate truly excited about the prospect of working there, and a direct way to do that is through using the job description to show the investment the organization places in each employee.

Phase 3: Building an Inclusive Interview Panel

The next step is for organizations to build inclusive interview panels to meet with and assess each candidate. Inclusive interview panels have gendered and ethnic representation across the panel and can be made up of individuals who are on the team that is hiring or from a cross-functional team who would work closely with the role in question. I've spoken with so many candidates who have shared with me that when they have attended interviews in which not one of the interviewees look like them, they take the answers they get about the organization's culture and workplace experiences with a grain of salt. I recommend that there be an even number of individuals on the panel to avoid neutral bias (attempting to achieve complete neutrality, which is highly unhelpful in the interview process), and there should be no more than four to six individuals on the interviewing team. This will ensure that there won't be an overwhelming number of interviewers but there are still enough different perspectives to be considered in making the decision to extend an offer.

Perhaps most important is that there should be a standardized process for every applicant and role. Every interviewer should know exactly what questions they are asking and what answers they are looking for before they step foot in the interview. These answers should leverage a rubric of preset ratings that will create a standardized numerical understanding of how the candidate performed based on the different parts of each of their answers. All candidates should also be given DEI-based anti-racist questions, and these questions should be broken into two categories: one for individual contributors and one for managers leading a team. These categories will be able to provide insight into the different responsibilities and expectations of each role. Here are some questions I recommend asking individual contributors:

- Please share an experience where you've amplified another person's voice on your team. Why did you have to do that? (This will enable interviewers to determine if they are bringing on an individual who can assess a dynamic and advocate for their colleagues if there is potential harm being caused, whether intentionally or unintentionally.)
- What is your approach to understanding the perspectives of colleagues from different backgrounds?
- How have you ensured diversity, equity, inclusion, belonging, and anti-racism were embedded in the work that you did? How did you measure those criteria and what was the impact?

Now for managers with direct reports, I recommend asking the following questions:

- How did you drive DEI efforts within your organization and how did you measure them? What was the impact?

- What power and privilege do you possess? How have you used that to drive efforts and empower those around you? (If the interviewee seems confused, the interviewer can provide an example of the power they themselves hold. For example, my power and privilege is even as Black woman, I had two parents that came to this country who were financially stable and had the ability to put me in private school. I was exposed to private school education and I watched the impact of how my career progressed with that level of power.)

It's possible that some candidates may not have had this experience in active DEI work. If they are struggling to provide answers, then the interviewers can encourage them to talk more about the things they've witnessed or changes they would be interested in driving. For entry-level candidates without extensive professional experience, the interviewers can broaden these questions to apply to previous coursework or internship experience. By standardizing interviews and embedding DEI-based questions into the behavioral portion, organizations will be able to gather a more holistic understanding of each candidate and will be able to build balanced and diverse teams.

Phase 4: Candidate Selection

Once all candidates have gone through the full interview process, the last step is to select the final candidates who will be offered a job. I strongly recommend that each stage of interview feedback be recorded as close to the interview as possible. It can be so easy to intend to complete interview feedback later in the day or week, but sometimes things come up and we forget, or the details get fuzzier the longer we wait. It is most equitable for all feedback to be recorded right after the interview so all information is as fresh and accurate as possible. Once it is time to make the determination, I recommend that the entire hiring team comes together to discuss their thoughts on the candidate. These conversations should include the hiring manager, the recruiter who has been speaking closely with the candidate, and all interviewers. Each person should have the opportunity to share their thoughts on how the candidate performed during the interviews and reference the standardized rubric for equitable scoring. Based on these discussions, the hiring team will be able to come to a decision on which candidates they would like to extend offers to.

Phase 5: Check-In

As the recruiting life cycle comes to an end, the employee life cycle begins its journey. The candidate goes from being an interviewee to receiving an offer to becoming a full-fledged employee. Even though the recruiting phase has been completed, that doesn't mean the relationship-building element has dissipated. I strongly encourage the recruiting team to schedule one-on-one check-ins with the new hire within the first month or two of them starting. This can be a great way to see if there are any questions the new hire has about the organization or their team and to make sure they feel supported and happy with their decision to join the organization. Most likely the hiring manager will be in regular communication with the new employee because they will report to them, but there is a powerful human element to maintaining touchpoints with the recruiter and other team members or cross-functional colleagues. It diminishes the feeling of a transactional process and demonstrates a deeper care and community that exists within the employee body. The relationships we build have the power to transcend our immediate situations and are capable of cultivating and flourishing. After all, we never know the twists and turns that life will throw at us, but the more we practice extending our arms to one another, the more hands there will be to catch us if we stumble.

Chapter 7 Exercise: Is Your Recruiting Life Cycle Inclusive?

When creating a job description, there must be standardized language across all job descriptions that clearly outlines the organization's values, responsibilities, and commitment to DEI. It's important that a job seeker is excited about your organization before even applying by understanding what your organization does, what it offers for its employees, what the job entails, and how they will actually be able to grow within the role.

In the following table, create an inclusive job description by writing out the details to the prompts in the far right column.

	JD Criteria	Description	Your Response
About Your Organization	What Are Your Company's Values, Responsibilities, And Commitment To DEI?	What is your organization's mission, values, and stance on DEI? This statement should be powerful.	
	Organization Benefits	What benefits and perks do you offer that will entice a job seeker?	

	JD Criteria	Description	Your Response
	Example of How Employees Have Used Company Benefits	How can you prove employees are happy and benefiting from working at your organization?	
About the Role	**Job Title**	Title of open role	
	Salary Range	Salary range you are paying for this position. Disclosing what the previous person in this role earned is a bonus.	
	Job Description and Day-to-Day Responsibilities	What does this role look like in the day-to-day? With whom does this position work closely, report to, learn from? What does this position benefit from?	

(Continued)

JD Criteria	Description	Your Response
Requirements	These criteria are non-negotiables needed to be successful in the role. Assess your requirements with the team and decide what is truly necessary. Avoid arbitrary years of experience or education if most of the learning will happen on the job.	Must execute on one DEI goal each year
What You'll Learn	Excite job seekers with what skills they will learn on the job.	
How You'll Grow	Describe the growth trajectory for this role and what success looks like.	

JD Criteria	Description	Your Response
Nice to Have	Here you may share any additional skills or experiences that will drive success in the role.	

Job Description Checklist
- Clearly outlined organization's values, responsibilities, and commitment to DEI
- Included salary range
- Used a tool to ensure standardized language, inclusive wording, and gender neutral terminology
- Outlined inclusive benefits and provided examples of how folks have used them
- Described the role in detail
- Outlined role responsibilities including a owning a DEI goal
- Described what one will learn on the job
- Described ways one will be able to grow personally and professionally

Interview Standardization Checklist
- Interview panel has equal representation from a gender, race, ethnicity, and level.
- Panel is aligned on which questions will be asked by whom and the appropriate responses to each question.
- Interviewers are equipped with the tools to give unbiased feedback.

- Interviewers understand their responsibilities to provide feedback in real time during and immediately after each interview.

DEI Interview Questions
Required Questions for Every Interview:

- At COMPANY NAME, one of our values is Inclusion. Diversity, Equity, Inclusion efforts are tied directly to performance, and all employees are responsible for one goal that is worked on for the year. These goals help us to drive representation, greater retention, and inclusion for all. How would you like to drive DEI efforts within your potential new team at COMPANY?

  Answer: Candidate is able to provide specific examples of how they aim to drive efforts rather than relying on company efforts, DEI team efforts, or people team efforts.

- In your previous role(s), what were your personal DEI efforts and what was the impact?

  Answer: Candidate can speak to individual efforts made, not company efforts. Examples: efforts made toward inclusive recruiting practices, team retention, amplifying others' voices, intentional recognition of others' contributions, efforts to help grow team skill sets, providing exposure opportunities, and so on. Candidates should share how they measured their impact.

Inclusive Hiring Questions for Managers with Direct Reports:

- What are the top three ways you have practiced inclusive leadership and what impact did it have on those around you?

    Answer: Candidate is able to provide concrete examples of how individuals on their team or individuals worked with cross-functionally were affected in terms of career progression; being seen, heard, and valued; recognition; addressing issues that come up for team members; providing exposure moments for direct reports; championing team efforts; and so on.

- How have you worked collaboratively in creating a diverse pipeline with your talent acquisition partner?

    Answer: Candidate is able to share ways they have worked to inclusively expand their team in previous roles by identifying gaps and working intentionally with their talent team to ensure there is equal representation in the pipeline and interview process

- As a leader, how do you ensure diversity, equity, inclusion, belonging, and anti-racism are embedded in the work that you and your team do?

    Answer: Candidate is able to share concrete examples of how they have practiced DEI principles in a team setting. Examples: discussed gaps (demographic gaps, skill gaps) with team members, created growth and development pathways for their direct reports, shared team contributions to leaders to ensure team recognition, ensured team members have space to be heard, created intentional spaces for sharing and relationship building, provided outlets during times of social trauma, and so on.

Inclusive Hiring Questions for Individual Contributors:

- **Scenario:** You're in a meeting and someone is shutting down someone else's idea or interrupting another person. What action would you take in the moment? Would you do anything at all?

  Answer: Candidate is able to provide steps of action that directly support the affected person and provides space for the affected person to speak from their perspective across multiple scenarios in a constructive manner.

For example, how would the candidate practice inclusion if the aggressor is

  o A manager in a team meeting setting?
  o A teammate in a social setting?
  o A leader in a town hall setting?

  Answer:

  o Candidate is able to identify the power they hold (how outspoken they are, their position in the organization, their knowledge and experience, their connections/were they referred to organization, decision-making power, a specific skill set they have, their identity).
  o Candidate is able to assess and identify their power as it pertains to those around them.
  o Candidate able to speak to the actions taken on a daily basis to ensure that space is provided for perspectives of systemically overlooked populations.

- How do you ensure Diversity, Equity, Inclusion, Belonging, and Anti-Racism are embedded in the work that you do?

  Answer: Candidate is able to provide steps of action they take and practice on a daily basis within any role they hold or have held. For example:
  o Checking in with team members
  o Joining/supporting employee resource groups
  o Attending workshops/growth opportunities in the DEI/Anti-Racism space

- What are qualities of a non-inclusive leader?

  Answer: Candidate is able to provide concrete examples of non-inclusive leadership either through personal experience or narrative. For example:
  o Leaders who foster an "us versus them" culture
  o Leaders who focus on blame and shame when performance metrics are missed or there is an urgent incident
  o Leaders who foster toxic positivity providing only surface-level compliments without taking the time and effort to invest in individual employees and their growth
  o Leaders who do not recognize different perspectives, workstyles, or identities that are actively present in the workforce (internally/externally)

8

Employee Resource
Strategy Groups

LET'S KICK THIS chapter off with a bit of self-reflection. I want you to ask yourself, do you currently like your job? I hope that your answer is yes! Now for those of you who answered yes, let me ask another question, do you currently love your job? If you are lucky enough to answer yes once again, let me pose a third question. Do you love your job enough that you would do it for absolutely no money?

(This is where I'd expect to hear crickets if we were doing this in person.) Well, if you are one of the infinitesimally few people on this planet who would be able to work a full-time job with zero pay, then I'd love to take you out for a drink and pick your brain on how you are able to accomplish such an astounding feat. But for most of us, even if you loved your work with all your heart, it would be hugely challenging to work full-time for free. My hope for you is that you at least like your job. But whether you detest your job, like it, or love it, there is the same underlying theme: that we work so that we can provide for ourselves. Simply put, people work because they want to get paid. Despite it being the status quo for over two centuries in our country, people should never, ever be expected or forced to work for free. That also extends to situations in which individuals take on additional responsibilities outside of their formal role, and *especially* when these responsibilities are providing immense benefit to the organization.

We've already discussed employee resource groups (ERGs) a few times. ERGs play a powerful role in shaping the culture of an organization. However, in thinking about the responsibility and impact that ERGs affect, I have rebranded them to employee resource strategy groups, or ERSGs. The efforts led by ERSGs should be incredibly strategy driven; from the programming they develop to each of the roles that makes up each leadership team, ERSGs operate with intention to maximize their impact. And let me tell you, ERSGs can make quite an impact! I have worked with ERSGs who have been able to successfully recruit 30% of the organization's hiring goals for the year and educate the larger employee body through learning and development programming by bringing in speakers, mentors, and coaches to help participants enhance what they bring to their current job function. I've also worked with ERSGs who were able to support a nonprofit that fed hundreds of elderly Asian Americans in New York City during the pandemic and had the nonprofit publish an article on the ERSG's contribution and how they sent volunteers to help deliver the food.

All of these situations strengthen and connect an organization, whether it be through positive business impact, helping professionally develop employees, or creating a safe, more inclusive, and respectful working environment. And in order for ERSGs to be able to attain these successes, their work must be valued, respected, and compensated. After all, it's easily evident that investing in ERSGs *is* investing in the business.

ERSGs: How Will You Know If You're Ready?

Now before creating ERSGs, organizations need to first determine that they are ready and able to meaningfully support these groups. There are three main questions an organization should reflect on before deciding to sponsor ERSGs: does your organization have the representation needed to create ERSGs, does your organization have funding allocated for ERSGs, and will your organization be able to offer top-down support?

Does Your Organization Have the Representation Needed to Create ERSGs?

The first thing to consider is if there is a strong employee desire to have ERSGs, and if there is, whether or not the organization currently has enough representation to meaningfully do so. If the organization population includes less than 3% of the intended ERSG population, then I recommend the organization should instead consider creating an inclusion committee as a precursor to creating ERSGs. The last thing we would want is for a group to be formed that doesn't have the people power to sustain and grow, and ends up "failing" due to lack of preparation and support. An inclusion committee could offer an alternative by focusing on programming related to certain areas of shared interest for employees, thus casting a wider net for participation.

Building this sort of a committee would enable a community of like-minded employees with overlapping passions to grow and develop. Programming could include learning & development, global events, or inter-organization community building. Most important, an inclusion community should be solution oriented and be able to take on actions and delegate work across the group while building representation within the organization so it could get to the point of supporting ERSGs. Another alternative to inclusion committees is to create intersectional ERSGs, but only if that is an option that employees genuinely would like and are interested in. For example, I have worked with an intersectional ERSG focused on the Afro-Latinx community that was able to develop meaningful programming tailored to the Afro-Latinx experience.

Does Your Organization Have Funding Allocated for ERSGs?

As we've been exploring throughout this book, DEI plays an important role in an organization's business success, from promoting psychological safety through inclusive and equitable policies to attracting and retaining the talent that powers the business. Therefore, the amount of money allocated to the DEI department should be comparable to that allocated to other departments. Organizations put money into what they think will have the biggest return, and truthfully, that should be their employees. After all, what organization can run successfully without its people? ERSGs are a direct way for organizations to invest in their people by giving them the power and resources to shape practices and opportunities within the organization.

I understand that DEI is a growing space, and sometimes these financial decisions need to be made a step at a time. With that in mind, organizations should at the very least allocate at least a quarter of the average budgets of other departments for DEI. So for example, if the average budget for departments was $200,000 a year, then the DEI department should receive no less than $50,000 a year. Remember this is a minimum requirement, and an organization should aim to compensate each department equitably. If the organization is not ready to do that, then unfortunately it definitely isn't ready to support ERSGs, and frankly it's a bit of a red flag overall. For an organization to decide not to invest a quarter of what they are investing in other departments into DEI shows they don't value the organization's people, they are ignoring them, and therefore they are perpetuating the disparities that exist within the organization.

The DEI budget would partially go toward compensating ERSG leaders for their time and the ERSGs themselves for events and programming. In order to truly be strategy driven, there must be a budget for ERSG programming, as well as compensation for people's work, so that they are able to meaningfully allocate their time to drive initiatives. ERSGs should receive no less than $5,000 a year for programming, though I have seen organizations that have found their ERSGs to be hugely impactful and choose to annually invest $25,000 in each of them. On top of ERSG budgets, each group leader will need to be compensated for the time they spend as part of their responsibilities, in addition to their regular salary. There are five roles that make up the core ERSG leadership team: president, VP, secretary, treasurer, and researcher. Each leader should receive the same hourly rate that is no less than $20/hour (the current average compensation for a program manager), and will have a maximum number of weekly hours that they are expected to work on the ERSG-related responsibilities. Presidents should spend a maximum of five hours a week on ERSG work, vice presidents should spend a maximum of four hours a week, and the remaining three roles should spend a maximum of three hours a week. This will ensure that all leaders are compensated equitably, but those who will have to spend more time on their duties will have that reflected in their compensation. If the organization is unable to provide this budget and stipend for each ERSG lead, then quite simply the organization is not ready to support ERSGs. Without fair compensation, organizations run the risk of high employee burnout. Especially as ERSGs commonly support systemically overlooked populations within the organization, there is an added layer of compounded unpaid labor and stress these individuals will have to carry on top of their regular day-to-day responsibilities that would end up being strongly counterintuitive to the primary goal of ERSGs helping drive equitable and inclusive practices.

Will Your Organization Be Able to Offer Top-Down Support?

Top-down organizational support means that all ERSGs need to be fully embedded into the organization's practices and policies to make sure they are given the proper space and support to be fully used by everyone in the organization. Organizational support is derived from the relationships across four main teams; executive leadership, talent acquisition, HR, and DEI.

Executive Leadership Support   In order for ERSGs to truly be successful, they will have to play a role in the larger organization and will require executive leadership and performance-level commitment. Organizations should ensure that all executives are willing to participate in ERSG programming and act as executive sponsors to drive visibility and support. Executives need to make it a priority to attend ERSG-sponsored events and set a precedent that will trickle down to their direct reports and their direct report's direct reports. On the flip side, if executive leaders do not prioritize ERSG efforts, that will easily cascade down the organizational chain as well. For example, if there is an important ERSG event, executives should make sure their teams clear their schedules and move around other meetings to ensure they can all attend the events.

Talent Acquisition Support   Each ERSG should have their own recruiting link that they can share with potential hires that they connect with. I recommend that each ERSG work directly with a talent acquisition partner to find out the number of applicants who applied through the link, the number of candidates who got interviewed, and any individuals who were hired through the ERSG's recruiting link. This recruiting partner will be the point person for each respective ERSG and will be focused on helping the group meet their recruiting goals.

HR Support   ERSG contributions need to be baked into performance reviews. If any individuals are acting as an ERSG lead on top of their full-time responsibilities, then it is critical that their contributions within their ERSG be both acknowledged and shared during performance reviews because their ERSG work is also providing an important business impact alongside their formal role.

DEI Support   As you can see, there are a number of moving pieces to creating and maintaining ERSGs. Therefore, there needs to be an employee whose designated full-time role is helping oversee ERSGs by providing guidance on their strategies, implementations, and impact. I recommend this individual be a part of the DEI team and report to the DEI program manager. This individual will help each ERSG determine the impact they each want to have, as well as how they will create measurable success from their initiatives. This person will play a critical role in ensuring ERSGs remain strategy driven and can provide helpful guidance when needed.

By taking the time to address these three areas, organizations will be able to ascertain if they are ready to create ERSGs and empower them to become self-sufficient communities that will drive long-term and sustainable impact within the organization.

Meet the ERSG Leadership Team

Now that the organization has determined it is ready to build and support ERSGs, it is time to start putting together the leadership teams that will drive each ERSG. As mentioned the core leadership structure should have the following five roles: president, VP, treasurer, secretary, and researcher.

These roles should be selected on an annual basis, and the person will participate for a full year. If any individuals end up leaving, then their spot would open up for re-election, and the next elected leader would finish out the remainder of the year. If the new leader came into their position with less than six months remaining in the year, then they would have the opportunity to remain in that role for the following year. I strongly recommend that leaders do not hold the same position for more than two years in a row because it is important that others have the opportunity to gain experience in different positions, which will also keep the election process equitable.

Each leader plays an important role in supporting the ERSG and has their own set of responsibilities.

President
- Oversees the ERSG's overall strategy and ensures all initiatives work in tandem with the organization's business goals
- Ensures all individuals are aware of their respective roles and responsibilities
- Acts as liaison with executives to engage them in supporting the group's initiatives
- Shares updates and reports monthly to executives and fellow ERSG leads on wins, challenges, and business impact
- Works with their team to develop an annual road map with respect to events and budgets and sets the cadence for programming
- Organizes and assigns subgroup tasks and offers guidance in the process.

Vice President

- Works closely with ambassadors, members, and new hires to ensure there is a structured process for joining and getting involved in group initiatives
- Acts as project manager by setting goals for ambassador subgroups and working closely with each subgroup to track progress and accomplishments
- Keeps up with ambassadors' efforts and contributions by tracking all progress on these initiatives and reporting feedback to ambassadors' managers on a quarterly basis
- Explores different creative ways to reward or provide recognition to the ambassadors for their hard work to encourage active participation

Treasurer

- Partners with the DEI team, finance teams, and leaders within the ERSG to set and adhere to the budget for the year
- Documents all invoices, receipts, and expenses in the ERSG budget sheet
- Is responsible for the ERSG credit card and will be the authorized user for any purchases or payments

Researcher

- Manages engagement by reaching out to folks individually on Slack to remind them of upcoming events to drive high participation
- Researches and identifies gaps that exist for the group through launching surveys and reporting on data for initiatives the ERSG is working on

- Builds transparency about identified gaps and the corresponding implemented solutions and outcomes
- Monitors the team's recruiting link and shares any interviews or hires with the ERSG on a monthly basis
- Records and assesses the success of every event and documents the data for the ERSG's business impact
- Provides the metrics and data necessary for ERSG leaders to make informed decisions on strategically driving successful engagement

Secretary
- Responsible for all documentation, content creation, and scheduling
- Sets up all-team meetings, schedules events on the ERSG-wide calendar, and sends reminders and updates for upcoming events
- Takes meeting notes and creates event flyers
- Responsible for the ERSG's blog posts, newsletter content and should record all information where the organization keeps its internal team workspace
- Shares updates on the ERSG externally as well via LinkedIn and other platforms to help attract new talent
- Ensures the ERSG recruiting links are being used in productive ways and brainstorms ways to engage more people and reach wider audiences for upcoming opportunities at the organization.

These five roles will be supported by ambassadors, who are volunteers within each ERSG who act as liaisons between the leadership team and the larger ERSG community and the rest of the organization. These ambassadors will amplify and share information on upcoming ERSG initiatives across the organization. Ambassadors will not get paid because they don't have consistent duties and are more present on a volunteer basis. This would be a great opportunity for folks who want to support specific projects but don't want to commit to a whole year.

In addition to ambassadors, there's still one more important player whom we need to meet. Each ERSG must have their own executive sponsor who will be the team's mentor at the individual and group levels. Executive sponsors are employees at the organization's executive level who will be paired with one ERSG every calendar year. I've seen some organizations assign two executive sponsors to each ERSG to enable every executive at the organization to get the opportunity to work with and support the ERSGs. These executive sponsors will get to know each of the five leads and help each of them grow within their role. The executive sponsors will be tasked with highlighting and advocating their ERSG's work to other senior leaders and making sure each lead's manager recognizes the contributions their respective report is making within the ERSG. Executive sponsors will be able to leverage their personal expertise and networks to help drive the ERSG's impact by connecting them to different individuals, tools, or organizations that can help support their efforts. They will also get performance reviews from the ERSGs leaders they work with so that their contributions to the ERSGs will also be documented. This will enable the executive sponsor to quantifiably demonstrate how they were able to help propel the ERSG leaders forward and help move the needle for the ERSG overall. After all, the greatest leaders I've been fortunate enough to work with were all great because of their ability to help those around them become great, thus enabling their impact to grow and multiply by positioning others to do the same as well.

Now that we have met the full leadership and sponsor team, the last piece I want to touch on is about creating an accountable and supportive environment for the leaders to collaborate within. First off, each ERSG should have access to centralized communication and literature to keep all operations organized and maintain consistent communication. I also recommend ERSGs maintain an inter-leader evaluation process that enables each leader to highlight each other's strengths and keep record of all contributions. The evaluation can include questions such as if each leader consistently attended and participated in meetings, if they were able to give notice for missed meetings, or if they carried out each of their respective responsibilities. This will enable each ERSG to keep track of their leader's efforts and wins, and ensure that the team is working together and supporting one another while driving impact.

The Three Pillars   So now that we've assembled our team of leaders, it's time to really put the *S* in ERSG and get to work! There are three pillars of focus and strategy that ERSGs can use to create their impact-driven road map. It's important to note that each ERSG will not have identical strategies, and each group will be able to determine their own missions and measurements of success based on the individual needs and interests of its employee body. This is a nonexhaustive list, but I have worked with ERSGs that have supported Black+, Latinx+, Asian+, Womxn+, LGBTQ+,

Middle Eastern+, veterans, caregivers, and differently abled communities. It can reasonably be inferred that each of these groups will have their own agendas and challenges they are seeking to address. However, no matter what each ERSG chooses to focus on, it can still be boiled down into three particular areas, which I call pillars.

The first pillar is focused on recruiting and retention. This pillar will heavily focus on general recruitment and retention of candidates or employees who identify as part of the ERSG's community. However, this can be taken a step further to also create tailored strategies to areas related to recruiting and retention that are relevant to each ERSG. For example, I've worked with a caregivers ERSG who wanted to focus on helping folks who had a gap in their work experience due to caregiving responsibilities. They led a résumé workshop to help individuals with this gap learn how to talk about their experience and use it as a strength in interviewing to make it easier for them to re-enter the workforce. It's important to remember that solutions can be creative, engaging, and specific to the needs and interests of the ERSG population.

The next pillar is growth and development. This pillar is focused on accelerating the development of ERSG members and will be a key area the executive sponsor(s) can support. I have seen executive sponsors build relationships with and assess individuals within the ERSG and then help them transition into other opportunities across the organization. For example, one womxn ERSG I've worked with was able to facilitate their secretary getting promoted to an executive assistant role because of the excellent work they did as an

ERSG lead. Identifying leaders within the ERSG has the potential to benefit the organization as a whole by illuminating impactful individuals who are interested and able to grow into leadership roles across the organization. Growth and development strategies can also target external communities as well. I've worked with a Hispanic/Latinx+ ERSG that developed a sponsorship program for folks within the Hispanic/Latinx+ community. The ERSG built a partnership with an organization focused on computer literacy for Hispanic/Latinx middle and high school students. Through this partnership the ERSG was able to sponsor students going through the program, as well as lead programming for the organization in professional development and job readiness. This opportunity gave the organization's employees an opportunity to meaningfully engage with their larger community while also providing mentorship opportunities for their own members.

The last strategic pillar is engagement and branding. This pillar will focus on strategies about how the ERSG chooses to promote their events both within the organization and externally. I strongly recommend that while developing and implementing these strategies, the ERSG works closely with the organization's communications department to use the expertise of individuals who primarily work within that vertical. This pillar also provides an opportunity for ERSGs to play a role in how the organization's product can inclusively engage with its audience. For example, one ERSG I worked with was focused on accessibility and wanted to add some features to their organization's product to increase its accessibility for different populations. They were able to collaborate with the product team to add an optional feature for color-blind users to the product's user interface. This initiative helped evolve the product into a more inclusive one and also enabled the ERSG to work with the product and design teams, which was a new opportunity for many members who did not work on a technical team. Building opportunity through synergy is just one of the many ways that ERSGs can drive meaningful impact within the organization.

With this framework in mind, ERSGs will be able to drive meaningful and quantifiable impact that will ripple into the organization's larger ecosystem. The primary goal that we started with at the beginning of this chapter was to develop self-sustainable employee-led groups that would continue to shape and support the organization's inclusion and equity practices. This becomes possible through the provision and investment of resources that can engage and empower leaders in the organization to have meaningful impact. That investment will require an allocation of financial resources, time, and leadership, but once set up you'd be amazed at what a group of motivated and impact-driven individuals can do. So if you take anything away from this chapter, let it be to pay your people and never underestimate what they're able to accomplish when they are invested in.

Chapter 8 Exercise: A Strong Support Structure Fuels High-Performing ERSGs

In order for ERSGs to reach their maximum potential, it's critical there is a structure in place to support them. This includes stacking the groups with full leadership teams, executive sponsors, and a team of supporting ambassadors to ensure groups have the people power to carry out initiatives that drive business impact. The goal for an ERSG structure is to have defined roles and responsibilities for three to five core leadership roles, supported by two executive sponsors who are at the senior director and above level, and at least three ambassadors. Organizations should only seriously consider forming ERSGs when they have the resources, representation, and support to do so. Use the following checklist to assess your organization's readiness:

- The organization has at least 3% of employee makeup of the intended ERSG population for a particular group.
- The organization can provide funding to each ERSG and compensate group leaders.
- The organization has support from the executive team, talent team, HR team, and a DEI leader.

Leadership Team Support Structure

Every ERSG should have their own leadership team with the support model shown in Figure 8.1.

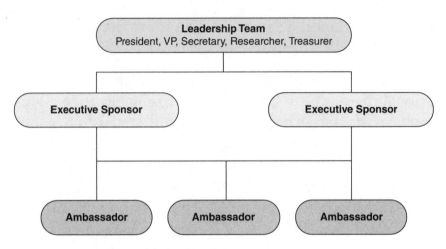

Figure 8.1   ERSG leadership breakdown.

Leadership Roles and Responsibilities

Every paid ERSG leadership position should have structured responsibilities and deliverables to execute.

President	The president is responsible for developing ERSG strategy, overseeing programming, and ensuring all ERSG leads are aware of respective goals, roles, and responsibilities. They advocate for their leadership team members, drive agendas, and are the core liaison to the group's executive sponsors.
Vice President	The VP is responsible for working closely with ambassadors, ERSG members, and new hires to ensure there is a structured process for joining and getting involved in group initiatives. The VP sets goals for ambassador subgroups and works closely with each subgroup to track progress and accomplishments.

Secretary	The secretary is responsible for documentation, content creation, and scheduling and managing calendars on behalf of the ERSG. The secretary also takes meeting notes and creates event flyers and blog posts or newsletters amplifying the work the ERSG is doing to publish internally and externally.
Researcher	The researcher identifies gaps that exist for the group, launches surveys, and reports on data for initiatives the ERSG is working on to ensure employees understand the importance, potential gap, and outcome. This person should help the ERSG dig deeper into topics, research data points, and track the effectiveness of programming via surveys or polls.
Treasurer	The treasurer is responsible for partnering with the people team and leaders within the ERSG to set and adhere to a budget for the year. This person submits invoices, receipts, and expenses, and documents spending in a budget sheet.
Executive Sponsors	Executive sponsors are ERSG leaders' advisors and support system and should assist in accomplishing and tracking ERSG goals and metrics. Sponsors can amplify the work leaders are doing internally; encourage more leaders to get involved; and can rely on their skill sets, strategies, personal networks, and connections to support the growth of the ERSG.

Ambassadors   Ambassadors are group members who volunteer to support ERSG initiatives and efforts. These are employees who want to be involved in the conversation but aren't taking as active of a leadership role. The president and VP can work together to assign ambassadors to specific initiatives or programming to carry out.

How Will This Structure Look at Your Organization?

ERSG support is most successful when leaders across various roles, functions, and departments are part of the process. Use the following chart to create a comprehensive list of leaders and teams who will be instrumental in supporting your ERSGs.

Role	Potential Leaders to Engage
Executive Sponsors (Senior director level to C-suite position leaders who will support group initiatives and provide strategy)	
Finance Team Leaders (Leaders to engage in compensation conversations)	
People Team Leaders (Leaders to engage in performance review conversations)	

9

Impactful Layoffs

IT'S THE START of a fresh workday. You woke up a bit earlier today and decided to go for a morning jog before your first meeting. After finishing your run, you get cleaned up and make yourself a fresh pot of coffee or tea and some toast. You pull your laptop out at your kitchen table as you prepare to go over new emails as you munch on your breakfast. But for some reason your password isn't working, and you can't log in to your computer. It's definitely strange, but you pull out your phone to check your work email and see if there was any notice from the organization or security team that would explain your difficulty logging in. To your shock, when you try to open your email you get a prompt saying the email account has been deactivated. Your mind starts racing, and you feel a growing panic. You don't want to believe it, you knew it was happening for organizations across all industries, but you never thought it would happen to you.

Layoffs are like a blindsided breakup. Imagine you are married and out of the blue your partner hands you divorce papers over your morning coffee. To top it off, you have to pack up all of your belongings under the watchful gaze of a security officer (now where did that person come from?!), and you're not even given the chance to say good-bye to your in-laws! It's shocking and heartbreaking, and you're having a hard time processing these changes as they are hitting you so fast your head is starting to spin.

This is the sad reality that people face every day. Organizations make the difficult decision to conduct company-wide layoffs, leaving behind those who will no longer be employed by their organization for reasons outside of their control. As much as people would like to think that business is business, the true fact of the matter is that all businesses have a level of humanness because there are humans at the core of it. Layoffs become necessary when an organization hasn't proactively implemented thoughtful economic financial projections, headcount alignment, internal transitional programs, and more.

It's important to note that not all layoffs are made equal. Some folks may find themselves in more challenging situations due to their personal life and financial responsibilities. I've worked with many organizations and leaders who have asked me about the best way to handle layoffs. Leaders have cried to me about the guilt they feel in having to lay off people. Some leaders offered to resign because they didn't feel they should continue in their role after having to make a decision that would have powerful consequences for many of their colleagues. If companies *truly* understood what it meant to be people first, they would look at every option before a layoff. Furloughs, wage reductions, cutting executive bonuses, whatever it would take to keep as many committed people on board as possible. In the event that layoffs indeed become necessary, there is still a strong opportunity for organizations to move through the process with empathy, thoughtfulness, and dignity for those whose time with the organization has ended. There is a way to balance the organization's needs with treating all those involved with respect.

You Can't Dig Yourself Out of a Hole That Hasn't Been Dug

Layoffs are categorized as instances when employees are let go for reasons outside of their performance or actions. If it weren't for these external reasons, these people would all remain employed. This is different from terminations, which occur when the employee's performance is not up to par, usually despite manager intervention and additional training. Layoffs are when the organization itself does not identify that the economy is shifting or the impact that shift will have on the organization's financial performance. As a result certain roles or teams have to be removed. Now I'm no CFO here; in fact, it's more than safe to say that math was not my strongest subject. That being said, something simply isn't adding up. Financial proofing should start way before an organization notices economic shakiness in order to avoid sizable shifts from occurring. However, there are a few things organizations can do to try and prevent these sizable shifts from occurring.

How to Avoid Layoffs

My observation is that organizations tend to undergo layoffs due to two main reasons. The first reason is when organizations are not moving in accordance with the market and make business decisions that cannot be supported by the current state of the market. The second reason is when organizations go through extreme hiring without a thoughtful and intentional long-term strategy. There have been many times when organizations have been affected by entirely external occurrences. We have seen recessions hit hard and cause organizations to downsize. We've lived through a pandemic in which business literally stopped for many organizations. When these types of events occur, the economy is hit with instability and organizations fight to weather the consequential rockiness. These are precisely the times in which organizations should be especially careful with the areas in which they allocate their budget. As these challenges are oftentimes unpredictable, organizations should always be prepared to ride out some bumps and have contingency plans for when financial targets are not met, instead of scrambling to find quick and temporary ways to recoup losses. On the flip side, sometimes we've seen the market seem to favor certain industries hit with rapid growth. For example, also during the pandemic, there was a massive increase in demand within the technology sector. As quarantines began to take effect, people needed a way to continue conducting their lives as normally as possible without leaving the house. This required a quick shift to digitized products that could be accessed remotely. From groceries to health care, industries needed to adapt and accommodate the requirements of the time. This led to a boom in the tech sector, leading some organizations to hire aggressively and grow dramatically. However, once the money stopped coming in and things began to equilibrate, these organizations had ended up growing beyond sustainability and were then forced to lay off large percentages of their workforce as they couldn't keep up with their rapid growth. It is *so* important that organizations are aware of and take into consideration the current market and align their business decisions accordingly so they can sidestep creating their own pitfalls.

Turning and Burning Employees

Have you ever witnessed an organization create a false sense of urgency about rapid hiring? I've seen multiple organizations receive substantial funding, only to follow it with extreme hiring that they end up unable to keep up with. Organizations should never hire for hiring's sake. It creates a misalignment between the current funding available for hiring and the number of roles actually needed. Even if organizations gain substantial funding, they should still always remain strategic in how they grow the business and the people they choose to bring in. If an organization is laying off 400 to 600 employees or more, that means they seriously missed their projections. It is unrealistic to think that endless growth will always be sustainable, so organizations should always strategize for the long run. When organizations don't do this, there can be a number of potential scenarios, the worst being people who have left other stable and well-paid opportunities to come to the organization only to be let go because of a previous lapse in financial judgment. I've also heard from individuals who were at organizations affected by layoffs and were shocked to see that there were still open roles on their organization's website. Why would the organization be hiring new employees when they just had to let go existing employees? Someone please make it make sense! And the easiest way to do that is to hire intentionally, conservatively, and with a shrewd eye on actual business needs.

Proactive Internal Partnership

When organizations are positioned to grow their employee base, the CFO and finance team should determine a realistic and logical headcount. They should assess if any current gaps exist in roles or job function, then work directly with DEI and the people team to assess which roles would provide substantial benefit and explore whether they can streamline these opportunities for employees who are already at the organization. The teams can work together to consider the impact that different managers or individual contributors have and figure out if it is possible to move these folks up to fill these gaps. If the finance team and CFO work in a silo, they won't get insight into which employees are really interested and capable of growing and taking on more responsibilities that will ultimately help drive the business's success.

After this discussion, the organization can then decide whether it's truly necessary to bring in more employees. If the demand calls for it, then the organization can decide to move forward with hiring, but I strongly urge that it does so slowly to prevent over-rapid growth and give the hiring teams time to keep their standards high in bringing in new hires. It's so important that organizations don't get ahead of themselves, because markets can sometimes be volatile and leave organizations scrambling to keep up. It's better that organizations take the time to be rigorously thoughtful in their business decisions.

Preparing for Empathetic Layoffs

Once an organization knows it is *that* time, there is a lot of prep work the organization should do to facilitate as smooth a process as possible. It needs to decide what roles and therefore individuals will be laid off, and in doing so it will be able to get an understanding of which roles cannot be laid off and may even need additional people power. In essence, organizations need to create a transition program that should be instituted long before a layoff is ever considered. This enables a flow of employees moving laterally or vertically across the organization based on business needs. In the event of layoffs, the transition program can then be leveraged to first shift employees in roles included in the potential layoff to find other roles at the organization without having to let them go. There may be other departments within the organization that could potentially take on some of those employees with overlapping skill sets instead of spending the time and money to hire externally. This will help the organization retain individuals who are doing well and contributing meaningfully to the organization by shifting their job functions but keeping them full-time. Why would an organization want to remove employees who are dedicated, loyal, and committed?

However, if the organization is unable to move these roles around and keep all employees, then it needs to come up with a game plan for every individual who is getting laid off. Organizations should seek to align with their clients or partnering organizations to assess who may have upcoming openings, and then make introductions on behalf of the laid off employees. This is an opportunity for organization leaders to highlight the work of these employees to their larger networks and demonstrate that these individuals would be an asset to whatever organization they are a part of. If I were ever to be affected by a layoff, I would hope that there would be more appropriate recognition on LinkedIn for my accomplishments and contributions. If my organization filled out a recommendation for me or helped connect me with new opportunities, it absolutely would make a huge difference! The organization should provide interview and résumé courses to help during the job transition and should also encourage remaining employees to feel comfortable reaching out to their respective networks as well and help with any connections or recommendations for their former colleagues. Just because these employees' time at the organization has come to an end doesn't mean that the community and relationships that were built simply dissipate. By keeping it a human-first process, it enables the layoff process to offer true support in the following steps.

Having the Tough Talks

But how should the actual conversation be handled? Organizations should always try to have one-on-one conversations led by the people team and with DEI present (keeping it inclusive!) to answer any questions and discuss severance packages. This will enable the organization to align its messaging and provide its employees with an opportunity to ask their questions on an individual basis. If a one-on-one conversation simply wouldn't be possible due to the sheer number of layoffs, then I recommend that these conversations be held on a team basis to spare the people and DEI teams from being tied up in these conversations until the next round of layoffs. Only kidding, but really—it's important that these conversations happen fastidiously and transparently. After these smaller conversations are held, then there should be a larger meeting with organization leadership because, honestly, at the very least these people deserve a conversation.

It'll also give the leaders a chance to address the situation and share how the organization will continue to support individuals in finding their next endeavors.

Personalizing Severance Packages

Severance packages are often provided in the event of layoffs to help lessen the financial blow of suddenly losing employment. Think of severance packages like car insurance. All insurance offers some level of support, but each policy has a different level of coverage. Now severance is usually based on seniority, but continuing with the insurance metaphor, I strongly recommend that organizations take this a step further and personalize the entire severance package. It is so important that organizations understand the complexities of layoffs and how they have the strong ability to affect all areas of a person and their family's lives. Organizations should always take the time to understand the employees they are letting go. Who are each of these people, and what are their unique situations? What needs do they currently have, what challenges will arise with this shift in employment status? Organizations clearly took the time to get to know each of their employees as they were interviewing as potential candidates, so there's no reason why organizations wouldn't take that same level of attention and care during a layoff. A lot of this information can be collected when employees join the organization. Organizations need to know at the very least whether an individual moved or relocated for the position, or if there are any financial, personal, or health considerations the employee has that need to be addressed as part of their severance package.

For example, one scenario that unfortunately became common during the pandemic was that when organizations shifted to remote work, people used it as an opportunity to move their families out to areas where quality of life was cheaper and they could have the flexibility to do more. Can you imagine the excitement of getting a new job that enables you and your family to buy a house (taking on a mortgage) and live in an affordable neighborhood? And then can you imagine the shock and fear if that job is suddenly rescinded, and now you're left with a huge mortgage and no income. It would be a terribly stressful situation for anyone, and organizations should leverage their layoff budget equitably to provide additional assistance or supplement severance packages for the employees that have specific financial needs such as these. No one deserves to lose their home over a layoff that was out of their control.

Another resource organizations need to offer as part of severance packages *must* be health insurance. For so many people, losing their health insurance could be the most frightening part of losing one's job. Furthermore, trying to go through the stressful job search process while dealing with health issues without any sort of coverage is just plain awful! Going through such a challenging situation can be incredibly difficult to bounce back from, so it's critical that organizations extend this level of empathy and understanding by embedding health insurance as part of the comprehensive severance package.

Leveraging DEI in Layoffs

Layoffs create a cultural reset, which can be for the better or the worse. If properly used, the DEI team can work to ensure that this cultural reset provides an opportunity for growth process refinement across the organization.

DEI needs to be embedded into the full employee life cycle, and that includes an employee's exit. Organizations place such an effort on building an inclusive organization, but those efforts can be easily ripped apart if DEI isn't considered during layoffs. Let's say, for example, that an organization has recently been making a push in the last few years to hire more diverse talent. Then, when layoffs arrive, the organization takes the approach of letting go the newest employees. This would have a massively detrimental impact if a significant portion of the employees of color were let go and be highly counterproductive to the inclusion efforts the organization has been making. In the event that layoffs are indeed the best thing for the organization, then it needs to make sure it's carrying out layoffs in a way that will have the best outcome for the organization. This includes considerations about how ERSGs may be affected by layoffs, and ensuring that ERSGs will still retain both leaders and representation in the wake of layoffs.

There is also substantial data that illustrate how overlooked populations are disproportionately affected by layoffs. This can point back to the intersections from high numbers of overlooked populations working in service, food, hospitality, or labor—industries that are hit the hardest during disasters. We saw this during the coronavirus pandemic, when the lockdown was enacted and people transitioned to working from home, that these were the industries that struggled the most from lack of in-person customers. As a result, the people working in these industries found themselves unemployed in the middle of an epidemic. Any sort of challenge or pressure will only widen the gaps that already exist, making it that much more important to be laser-focused on these inequities and proactively working to mitigate them as much as possible when faced with difficult business decisions.

It's also important to note that when layoffs hit, DEI is one of the most commonly affected departments. As I mentioned, if layoffs are conducted based on seniority, and DEI is one of the newest departments to join the workforce, it becomes quite an unfortunate correlation. These organizations will then have to learn firsthand how very counterproductive it was to remove any members of the DEI team, because the organization will have to turn right back around and hire someone new to maintain integral programming and policies that strongly contribute to an organization's overall health and stability. Furthermore, as we've established, DEI plays an important role in navigating layoffs, from the conversations they facilitate to headcount determination and supporting transitional programming, let alone all the other impactful initiatives DEI drives day-to-day. If DEI is let go, who is going to actually help the organization recover from the layoff?

How to Move Forward Together

At this point we've explored the different considerations organizations should take while navigating layoffs. But did you think I was going to forget to focus on the remaining employees in the organization? The ones who made it through the layoff but are now scared as heck for their jobs and future at the organization? Well, if I had, that wouldn't be truly inclusive now, would it? Granted these folks may not have been directly hit by the layoff, but they are still very much affected by it! They might be unexpectedly saying good-bye to professional relationships or friendships they built over their time working together. They might be feeling a sense of shock and unease, a fear that they could be next. Some people report feeling survivor's guilt and may distance themselves a bit from the organization. Who gets laid off, and how they get laid off, has strong implications for those who remain. After all, even for those employees who weren't laid off, I'm sure they still would want to know how the laid-off employees were supported by the organization. If you found out your organization laid off your colleagues and didn't provide them with any sort of support or understanding, I'm sure that would leave you side-eyeing the organization a bit. After all, if the situation played out a bit differently, that could have been you who was dropped by your employer without any notice or empathy. But if you knew that those people who were laid off were given generous severance packages, health insurance coverage, and introductions to other job opportunities, I think it's safe to say that you might have some level of appreciation for the care the organization took in navigating a challenging situation.

It's important that leadership have transparent conversations with the remaining employees about the layoff and the steps taken by the organization to lessen the blow to those affected. It's critical to remember that communication is an important way to rebuild trust, and employees should feel protected in discussing what has transpired. It can feel terrible for employees and send a problematic message if the organization wants to sweep the layoff under the rug and not allow people to talk about it or how it affected them. What happened, happened, and it sucked. But there are still ways to move forward with empathy.

I urge organizations to use this as an opportunity to reset the organization's culture. Focus on identifying a new purpose-driven strategy and aligning the organization on it. Provide opportunities for employees to share their thoughts and ideas; after all, each person plays an important role in the organization's ecosystem and likely has a level of awareness of the challenges that could have led to a financial decline with the organization. Let the people who understand these issues best present potential solutions, and hear them out. The weeks following a layoff can provide a time to evaluate the organization's current culture and areas of improvement so that the entire organization can move forward together. Although layoffs are never easy, there are still ways to bring compassion, thoughtfulness, and humanity to the situation through leveraging a proactive layoff plan, and that is a huge part of being an accountable and inclusive leader. The very least an organization can and should do is provide the best level of support possible to those who were negatively affected and help them remain on their feet through a difficult transition. After all, it's what you would hope would be done for you, isn't it?

Chapter 9 Exercise: Are You Prepared to Make Impactful Layoffs?

Answer the following questions to assess whether or not you are ready to make inclusive layoffs.

Are Layoffs Your Last Resort?

As an organization, have you explored all options to furlough individuals instead of resorting to layoffs?	☐ Yes ☐ No
As an organization, have you explored all options to reduce wages instead of resorting to layoffs?	☐ Yes ☐ No
Before resorting to layoffs, have you assessed roles that are still active on your job boards to ensure existing employees aren't left without an opportunity to continue working at your organization?	☐ Yes ☐ No
Before resorting to layoffs, have your leadership and executive teams explored the option of decreasing annual bonuses?	☐ Yes ☐ No

Are You Prepared For Inclusive Layoffs?

Are you planning to continue hiring after proceeding with layoffs?	☐ Yes ☐ No
As an organization have you sought insight into which employees are interested and capable of growing and taking on more responsibilities that will help drive success?	☐ Yes ☐ No
Have you worked directly with your DEI and people teams to assess any potential gaps and whether or not opportunities exist for employees who are already at the organization?	☐ Yes ☐ No

Have you worked with your DEI team to assess communication and transparency of the layoff process?	☐ Yes ☐ No
Have you instituted a transitional program that allows a flow of employees to move laterally or vertically across the organization based on business needs?	☐ Yes ☐ No
Do you have an action plan for every individual who will be affected by the decisions?	☐ Yes ☐ No
Have you aligned with your clients or partnering organizations to assess who may have upcoming openings and made introductions on behalf of the future laid-off employees?	☐ Yes ☐ No
Have you provided interview and résumé courses to help during the job transition for those affected?	☐ Yes ☐ No
Are you able to offer inclusive severance packages? If not, then you have shared other opportunities for affected employees?	☐ Yes ☐ No

Are You Ready to Move Past Your Layoffs?

Have you created a leadership action plan to rebuild trust?	☐ Yes ☐ No
Have you created transparent and meaningful messaging to share with existing employees?	☐ Yes ☐ No
Have you shared your layoff action plan with employees so they are aware of the various benefits that have been offered to those who were affected?	☐ Yes ☐ No
Have you shared a purpose-driven strategy and communicated it clearly to employees?	☐ Yes ☐ No

Will employees have an opportunity to share their thoughts and ideas? ☐ Yes ☐ No

Do you have opportunities for employees to share their thoughts on rebuilding culture and participating in the organization in a new way? ☐ Yes ☐ No

10

Don't Retire Yet

I WANT TO retire early. No seriously, that's why I have 10 side hustles (ha)! And who wouldn't want to retire early? You probably want to retire early, too! However, as it relates to DEI, we simply can't just yet! I believe you will retire eventually, but it requires you not to retire yet. Instead, I want to encourage you to take all the knowledge and skills you gained through reading this book, and start really thinking about the places in which you notice similar gaps that could be solved by leveraging similar solutions. From learning how to build comprehensively supportive employee life cycles, to developing meaningful internal and external learning and development opportunities, to sponsoring ERSGs that can power and solidify powerful and inclusive practices—you now have the power to change the way your organization prioritizes, uses, and embeds a DEI framework.

Now, it's your turn! I want you to fill in the commitment petition at the end of this chapter that states you will not retire from DEI work yet, take a photo, tag me (Netta

Jenkins), and post it on LinkedIn. Let's create a movement together to ignite more folks to take action! What's even better is that you won't need to do it alone. Use what you've learned to fire up those around you so that you can come together and multiply your impact. However, I do recommend you make your life a little easier and just recommend this book to each of your colleagues so they can explore it for themselves.

Leadership is a behavior that can be found at any level, not a position. Ensuring an inclusive organization with leaders who operate from a people-first perspective can be driven by individuals at any professional level. That means understanding the gaps, disparities, and complexities faced by employee populations as a whole. So often organizations focus on business performance as an indicator of how the organization is doing. However, we've seen time and time again that business performance can't happen without the people who are driving the heart of the work. Organizations should think about keeping their people interested, informed, involved, and therefore inspired. This book is a hugely helpful tool that does just that—aiding leaders in understanding accurately what policies, practices, and resources are most meaningful and engaging for their employees so their employees are able to show up every day and give their best effort.

But, really, who would I be if I just gave you this information and told you to run with it without actually helping you piece together this future road map? In order to create these customized building blocks to help you derive solutions for your unique situations, let's do a quick refresher on everything we've covered so far. As we walk through each of the chapters, I encourage you to think about how each topic applies to your workplace, and how you can use these solutions to fit each of your needs. Fill out the commitment petition at the end of the chapter once you have created this detailed and personalized plan, and share it on LinkedIn (don't forget to tag me!). Let's get this movement started!

Chapter 1: Decoding Human Behavior

A lot of the behaviors that we see every day have strong historic roots. Though the basis of these roots can sometimes get lost throughout the centuries, it is imperative that we do our own due diligence and understand the full context of our behaviors and practices so we can determine what actions we should leave in the past and what we want to bring forward with us that will help create equitable and inclusive futures. As the workforce continues to globalize and we see careers evolve to fit modern workplaces, it serves organizations to provide the space for each of their employees to be seen as unique, comprehensive individuals. Organizations can't solve gaps that they can't see, and they can't see gaps if they don't give space for different dynamics, backgrounds, or cultural backgrounds. Once these gaps have been identified, the organization has three options of action:

- Completely ignore any gaps and run the strong risk of building an inequitable, homogenous, and exclusive culture that will be sure to have business repercussions.
- Provide performative actions where things may be addressed verbally but no structural change occurs.
- Put its money where its mouth is and take the time and (financial) effort to create impactful policies and practices that make the workplace more equitable and inclusive.

Chapter 2: Who Let the Dogs Out?

One of the most important ways an organization can get a pulse on its employee satisfaction is by going directly to the source to ask! However, just because an organization asks their employees how they are feeling doesn't mean that the organization will get honest and truthful responses. Why might that be? It usually has to do with the fact that these organizational surveys do not remain as anonymous as they are touted to be. For example, even if an employee's name isn't attached to the survey response, other demographic information such as gender, race, ethnicity, or job title could easily point to the respondent. This is especially true for overlooked populations who may not make up the majority demographic on their team. Therefore, instead of using your run of the mill company survey, I recommend working with third-party vendors who specialize in developing custom-ized actionable steps for the organization to take by collect-ing unbiased and strategically targeted questions that will uncover the presence of any gaps or inequities faced by any part of the employee body. These vendors are able to gain a level of transparency into current culture in a way that would be most difficult for an organization to accomplish through internal practices. Because it is conducted through a third party, these vendors are able to collect comprehen-sive data to aggregate into trends that will be meaningful for organizational strategy without giving insight into any one person's view.

Chapter 3: Franchising the Framework

Drawing from my own life experiences as a young middle schooler dealing with an unpleasant and ignorant bully to a young professional joining the corporate workforce, I've created a DEI framework that derives from three main areas of focus to increase overall productivity, performance, and profit. The Three Ps comprise people, practice, and product and touch on the foundation of an inclusive organization. I have said it before and I'll say it again: people are organizations' greatest assets and should be their primary focus. Organizations can heavily leverage DEI programs as well as ERSGs to drive initiatives that will support the people side. Practice comes when organizations take their DEI work beyond lip service and actually build and integrate long-term and sustainable DEI policies into their company practices and strategies. This could look like emphasizing supplier diversity and intentionally building partnerships, creating accountability measures to standardize inclusive practices throughout the full employee life cycle, as well as developing equitable reimbursement policies. Finally, although product is a newer frontier in DEI, it is also very exciting. DEI-specific applications can be used to strategize, measure impact, and promote transparent accountability that will help drive and organize DEI efforts across entire organizations. These three pillars work together to revolutionize how DEI gets embedded into everyday experiences in the workforce.

Chapter 4: The Most Underrated Leader

Because DEI is a relatively new field for many organizations, even though it was birthed out of the Civil Rights movement and ignited in corporate America in the late 1960s. Many organizations are still getting familiarized with how to develop impactful and effective DEI initiatives. However, we are quickly seeing how critical DEI is to the workforce in driving recruitment and maintaining retention; it is also quickly becoming apparent how important DEI leaders are to an organization's success. This chapter walks through the comprehensive steps that should be taken when developing a DEI department, from creating the actual expectations and job description for the DEI positions to how to interview and select the best-suited candidate. I share some common pitfalls to avoid and how to strategically think about the organization's DEI needs in developing the department from the ground up. Once the DEI roles have been filled, I also provide insight into how this new team should start to build rapport and trust with the rest of the organization to achieve their 90-day goals. This plan goes step by step to help organizations build a sustainable and empowered DEI department that will be able to derive clear and measurable goals.

Chapter 5: Sustainable Learning: Upgrading Your Learning and Development—MapQuest Directions to Google Maps

In order for organizations to develop inclusive and equitable career mapping to all employees, they must incorporate L&D programming for all employees at every level. L&D is solution-oriented programming to help develop employees and equip them to achieve their professional goals. This includes managerial training to assist managers in building customized career planning for each of their reports. We follow two main career pathways, one for individual contributors and one for managers. I lay out the broad responsibilities for each respective pathway at the associate, mid, upper, and C-Suite levels, as well as the expectations that need to be met in order to move up a level. Organizations that don't have these pathways explicitly outlined run the risk of inequitable promotion practices that can lead to lower retention rates. By providing clear expectations and trajectories, organizations make the internal growth process more transparent and accountable to help employees grow and stay engaged within their role.

Chapter 6: Are Your Policies Powerful or Powerless?

Policies are an incredibly powerful tool in increasing employee satisfaction and retention. There are four main areas to consider in developing policies that will have the most comprehensive benefit for the entire employee population: flexible policies, health care policies, policies to support caregivers, and growth and development. Flexible policies give employees the opportunities to align their work to their personal needs. This includes flexible hours and work-from-home practices, as well as direct reimbursement, which saves employees from taking on an additional financial burden, even if it is temporary. Health care policies extend from physical health to mental health, with the option for telehealth to support digital resources. Caregivers, for family members from all generations, may need additional support for family planning, childcare, and family leave. They should be fully supported in keeping up with their professional responsibilities as well as navigating their familial ones. Growth and development policies ensure that employees are able to expand on their interests and skill sets and are able to grow in ways that are meaningful to them. Organizations can work directly with their employees to ascertain which policies are most meaningful to their employees and within the financial budget. These policies have the potential to fluctuate with employee interest so organizations will assess the policies annually to keep their benefits competitive.

Chapter 7: Diversity Recruiting

If organizations are serious about their inclusion efforts, these efforts need to be practiced with humility and consistency. Diversity recruiting means developing a comprehensive recruiting strategy that seeks to mitigate any gaps or exclusion, especially for overlooked populations. This starts with building a proactive pipeline through intentionally developed relationships to create pathways for different demographics to enter into the recruitment stream. This can be achieved through developing and highlighting meaningful benefits that are geared toward improving equity for the employee body, cultivating diversity suppliers, or creating sponsorship programs that connect executive leaders with interested employees from overlooked backgrounds. We also discuss the proper recruitment life cycle, from deriving an accurate headcount, to creating an inclusive job description and interview process and panel, as well as selecting candidates who will be positioned to support business goals and grow substantially in the open roles.

Chapter 8: Employee Resource Strategy Groups

ERSGs can be a powerhouse of driving strategic inclusive organizational practices when properly supported, funded, and compensated. Before an organization decides to sponsor ERSGs, it must first be sure that it has the proper employee interest and funding needed for the ERSG to be effective. ERSGs should each receive a budget they can use for programming, events, and community building. There should also be a concerted leadership team made up of a president, vice president, secretary, treasurer, and researcher. It is imperative that each of these leaders is compensated equitably for the hours they spend on their ERSG responsibilities. In order for ERSGs to maximize their impact, they must have support from executive leadership, talent acquisition, HR, and DEI.

Chapter 9: Impactful Layoffs

Layoffs are a challenging and demoralizing process that are never easy for anyone involved. Although there are some strategies organizations can employ to stay financially stable, sometimes layoffs are unavoidable from unforeseen external pressures that require an organization to downsize. However, it is still possible to conduct layoffs with compassion, empathy, and meaningful support to those involved. Organizations should always have contingency plans in order for when financial goals aren't met to mitigate the number of layoffs. This can include transitional programs to internally shift people power to needed areas, deriving conservative headcount numbers based on what is required for business strategy, and creating pipelines to other opportunities by leveraging the organization's network. The organization should also create personalized severance packages that address each employee's financial situation and includes elements such as continued health care coverage and supplemental financial assistance for employees who have specific financial needs. It is also critical that organizations take this shift as an opportunity to actively rebuild trust with their remaining employee population and push the organization into a more transparent and unified space so that employees are able to feel valued and secure within their roles and the organization is able to move forward all together.

Chapter 10 Exercise: DEI Commitment Petition

It's your turn to build an inclusive organization! Following is a commitment petition that states you will not retire from DEI work yet. There is power in numbers, and together we can create a powerful DEI movement to ignite even more people to take action. I encourage you to use the following DEI commitment petition as a way to ignite change within your organization through the signatures and voices of you and your colleagues. You cannot have an inclusive organization without inclusive leadership. *You* are that inclusive leader and *you* spark the #DEIMovement within your organization!

DEI Commitment Petition

We, the employees of _____, commit to building a DEI road map for our organization that acknowledges historical disparities, focuses on inclusive leadership and hiring, develops growth plans for every individual, and implements people-first policies. We understand that prioritizing DEI policy and initiatives provides psychological safety in the workplace and educates people at all levels to become more inclusive leaders. We petition _____ to become an inclusive organization.

Name	Email Address	Signature

There is *power* in numbers, and conversations about inclusion are ever evolving! Once your petition is complete, take a photo of you and your colleagues to post on LinkedIn and tag me (Netta Jenkins) with the hashtag #DEIMovement so we can keep the conversation going and share this movement with others. Please also get in touch with me through my website, www.holisticinclusionconsulting.com. I can't wait to hear from you!

Acknowledgments

I THANK GOD for injecting knowledge, love, and action for humanity in my heart. This gift has attracted incredible humans and has laid the foundation for a wonderful community of movers and shakers all over the world who are dedicated to creating a shift in their respective ecosystems. These individuals see DEI work as a daily practice and seek to continue educating themselves to take real action. And, of course, my deepest gratitude and respect to those who came before us and fought the good fight, laying the path that we must continue down. I also need to extend warm thanks to a few special individuals who have played pivotal roles in my personal journey. These leaders have believed in my expertise, trusted me, invested in me, and remain my greatest champions. Many warm thanks to my former manager, Deb Josephs; Former Google and IAC HR executive, Gary Hoberman; former CIO for Metlife and current CEO of Unqork, Tim Allen; CEO of Care.com, Marc Lore; former CEO of Walmart and founder of Telosa, David Sullivan;

executive coach, Jane Tran; former COO of Unqork; and Jon Mallon, CEO of Telosa. I also need to thank my incredible team members Jacinta Mathis, cofounder of Dipper, as well as Harmony Richman, Abbie Szabo, Christopher Joyce, and Pam Benjamin. Thank you to every writer/reporter who has amplified my work publicly, especially *Forbes* contributor, Dr. Janice Gassam.

About the Author

Netta Jenkins IS a doctoral student and a leading voice in the diversity, equity, inclusion, belonging, anti-racism field, whose soaring 250k+ LinkedIn audience engagement played a key factor in *Forbes* naming her as one of the top seven Anti-Racism consultants in the world. She has also given a ground-breaking TEDx Talk, "Reimagining the Workplace."

Netta has been advising corporations and audiences of all kinds for more than 15 years on the most effective strategies to address systemic gaps in the workplace through her company, Holistic Inclusion Consulting. She cofounded Dipper, a review and ratings platform for professionals of color, and as a result was listed as one of LinkedIn's Top Voices for Equity in the Workplace in 2020. Netta has been featured in *Black Enterprise, Forbes, Business Insider*, and on CNN for her work and has won multiple awards for her impact in corporate and startup diversity. She was also included in *CIO Views* publication as "The Top 10 Most Influential Black Women in Business to Follow in 2021."

Currently, Netta serves as vice president of global inclusion for Unqork, a technology organization, and is an advisory board member for Betterment, an online investment company. Prior to joining Unqork, Netta created and executed strategy for five years as vice president, global inclusion for IAC/InterActiveCorp (NASDAQ: IAC). Netta is also working with Marc Lore, former CEO of Walmart to build the most inclusive city in America: Telosa, the first new city to be built in the United States in over a century.

The Inclusive Organization draws on Netta's background in communications, leadership, and behavioral psychology to create tailored DEI road maps for organizations to create more equitable workplaces.

Index